The Amazing Mr. Beam

The Amazing Mr. Beam

Greg Henderson

Strategic Book Publishing
www.sbpra.net

For information about special discounts for bulk purchases, please contact Strategic Book Publishing, Special Sales, at bookorder@sbpra.net.

ISBN: 978-1-63410-227-8

To my entire family

Acknowledgment

To Gordon Henderson and Joyce Henderson, my parents, who recently passed; my sister, Cindy, her husband, Mike, and son, Allen; of course, Mr. and Mrs. Beam, Karen, Joey, Zac, Cassie, Kadin, Kinlie Jo—all of whom mean so much to me.

To my gifts from God, my son Alex, my son Gabe, and his wife, Hannah, and my first grandchild born in February 2016, Gamble Gordon Henderson (or G4, as I am already calling him).

I would like to thank Hospice of Marshall County, the many angels who work there, helping people leave this world in peace, and to my Facebook friends for giving me the encouragement to do this. As a man of faith, I want to thank God for the blessings he has given me, especially the blessings of family and for entrusting me with His precious jewel Kathy. To Kathy I give special thanks for saying yes to that first date and then a second and also for allowing me to follow all of my crazy dreams and then living through them with me.

Thank you, Sharalee Sherman, for helping make all this possible.

God bless.

Contents

Prologue

Mr. Beam—the Beginning (at Least for Me)

I remember that Friday evening in March of my senior year in high school. I had a plan. I knew what I wanted to wear. The green pants, the melon silky shirt, and the white vinyl jacket with blue crossed tennis racquets on the left chest. I also wore the taller shoes, the ones with the two-inch heels. I had to look sharp because it was my first date with the cute little blonde, a sophomore. My attire had to be green because it was Saint Patrick's Day. I don't really celebrate the day much. I do think some of my ancestors were from Ireland. Our family tree on my mom's side tells the story of how the Heards came to the United States. It seems that one of my great-great-great-grandfathers living in Ireland got mad at a Roman Catholic priest and threatened him while chasing him with a pitchfork. The authorities did not take kindly to that and were looking to seize him when he fled by ship to the United States. I am sure he got asylum of some sort in Georgia (the debtor's colony), and eventually the family made their way into Alabama. None of that has anything to do with this story other than I have always found it interesting and slightly comical.

I proceeded to Howard Avenue in my mom's 1976 Mercury Bobcat. As I arrived at the door, I was a bit nervous, as always, but felt I could meet parents as well as the next guy. I confidently introduced myself to the smiling Mr. and Mrs. Beam, and we exchanged pleasant greetings. I cannot remember, but knowing them now, I am sure they had to be wearing matching clothes. My focus was on the lovely older daughter of Mr. Beam, the daughter we will call Kathy. We left, and I knew, this being our first date and Kathy being a sophomore, that it would be an early evening. A lot of the girls I dated had early times to be home, and then we would go in and watch television for a little while. We chose to go see the movie *American Hot Wax*, the story of Alan Freed, the Cleveland disc jockey who introduced rock and roll to teenagers in the late 1950s. There was also a *Woody Woodpecker* cartoon, which was pretty cool and the last cartoon before a movie that I remember seeing. The movie was over at about 9:00 p.m., and I thought we would drive over to the Sonic for a twist. A twist was both the vanilla and chocolate machine ice cream swirled together in a cone or a cup. After eating the twist, Kathy mentioned that she had to be home at ten.

Man, I thought, *she must be having an awful time to make up something like that.* I knew that she had a strong church upbringing and hoped it was a case of parents not liking for her to be out with someone whom they did not know, but ten o'clock? I had never heard of such. We made the seven blocks' ride in about, oh, three or four minutes, and then I pulled back into the same driveway where the evening began. I sat there for a moment, thinking that she might ask me in, but that did not happen. Suddenly, the porch light started going on and off, on and off, fast and then faster. I thought the whole neighborhood transformer might blow at any moment.

Kathy, reaching for the door handle, said, "I gotta go. That's my dad telling me to come in."

I did not know what to say or do, so I did not do anything. I did not get out and walk her to the door and did not open her car door. I just kept staring at the light going on and off as if I was in a hypnotic trance and the hypnotist, Mr. Beam, was telling me to go away. It was one of the most awkward endings to any date that I had been on, but it turned out to be the first of the many interesting ways of the amazing Mr. Beam.

As I write this compilation, Kathy and I have been married for almost thirty-three years. Many times, we had mentioned that we hoped to one day take her parents with us on some of our excursions, specifically Hawaii, which we did in 2014; and hopefully, if you decide to turn the pages, you will read about other adventures, which include New Hampshire, Maine, Washington, DC, Annapolis, and family gatherings. The Beams have been fantastic in-laws to me. They have not interfered with or criticized our parenting of sons, Gabe and Alex, nor our church choices, but have been supportive in actions and, I am quite sure, prayer as our family made our way through life. In addition to those mentioned so far, you will read about Gabe's wife, Hannah; the Beam's other daughter, the one we will call Karen, and her husband, Joey (the favorite son-in-law); their children Zac and Cassie, her husband, Kadin, and their daughter, Kinlie Jo. Ours is a typical Southern family that loves God and tries to enjoy this life and be kind to their fellow man.

I placed many of the following stories on Facebook for fun. The comments at the end of the stories from friends all over encouraged me to keep up the writing. Some of the comments are every bit as funny as the stories themselves. As I have told many people over the last couple of years who ask about Mr. Beam, all you really have to do is observe him living life, and stories jump out all around.

Squirrels! Squirrels! Squirrels!

Author's note: Mr. and Mrs. Beam, at the writing of these stories, were retired and in their seventies. In this story, there is a reference to a present you will read about a little later. Both Mr. and Mrs. Beam are mild-mannered, law-abiding, churchgoing, and never-hurt-a-fly people. Joey, mentioned at the end, is my childhood friend and now brother-in-law. He is the pastor of a fast-growing Albertville church, and I refer to him as the favorite son-in-law of the Beams.

Mr. Beam and the Battle for the Backyard

After retiring from the wild world of Wayne Poultry as a supervisor, watching chicken after chicken slowly make its way to evisceration, Mr. Beam eagerly planned to set up his backyard as a place where he and Mrs. Beam could spend many hours watching the amusing antics of beautiful, feathered friends for years to come. The first step was easy, as the sweet water-filled feeder attracted many amazing hummingbirds to the window over the sink, adding enjoyment to the time they both spent in the kitchen. But as with so many of us humans, Mr. Beam soon longed for more entertainment. Day by day, the backyard was transformed into a virtual haven for all kinds of birds. Ten, twenty, and then thirty bird feeders were added with all kinds of seeds and nuts. There were several birdbaths, that I am sure were imported from all over the world (well, maybe from local yard sales, but humor me here). There was one that you even plugged in, making a bird Jacuzzi. It was like a trip to the tropics for the bird population, an all-inclusive smorgasbord of seed and nuts, enough housing for hundreds of birds, most with views of the lush foliage of the one-and-a-half-inch-high lawn, thick, lush ferns, God-painted flowers, and the beautiful clear water of the birdbaths and spas. The Beams were ecstatic as the birds played for hours on end.

Then it happened. As with so many great places, the bad started to creep into the bliss. It is usually subtle at first, as was the case when Mr. Beam found the first feeder in shambles. It seemed that it was not a big deal; maybe a rogue squirrel had slipped in and had a little snack. Just like the storytelling warbling of the birds had spread the word of the oasis, the uncanny communication of the vermin world produced an onslaught of squirrels to their newfound playground. To top it all off, they got the added bonus of an enraged retiree trying all the well-known, squirrel-resistant tricks. None of this stopped the acrobatic squirrels from inventing ways of obtaining nuts and seeds while digging up the backyard vegetation. They would chew through wood and even metal. The daughter we will call Kathy entered the area, hopeful of figuring out a solution. After hearing something in a birdhouse, she cautiously opened the door. Large eyes, big teeth, and a bushy tail sprung toward her, running down her arm and leaping toward the sky. The tennis player's quick reflexes eluded the rodent, which proceeded to fly past her—yes, fly. The ever-dangerous flying squirrel was dive-bombing the relatives.

After Santa delivered the new secret weapon, Mr. Beam became locked and loaded, ready to reestablish control of the bird sanctuary. He began to open fire on the unwelcome guests. There was a problem: Mr. Beam was not the best shot in town or his block, or yes, even in his own house. For, try as he may, he could not even graze one of the speedy targets. The squirrels soon began to taunt him. Some would even seemingly pose very near to the man, as if Mr. Beam was working as a nature photographer.

One such squirrel was doing just that, aligned straight ahead, still eating a sunflower seed and staring at Mr. Beam, when Mrs. Beam excitedly encouraged, "Shoot it, Jerry." While he was fumbling for the gun, she said, "Give me that."

She grabbed the air rifle and fired one shot. The squirrel was sent flipping into the air and out on the ground. She then looked up at another squirrel some thirty feet off the ground on a branch in a tree and took fire, and the squirrel did not move ever again. Annie Oakley Beam was taking back the backyard. Now she was laughing with a bit of a sinister side that most of us never knew existed. She began doing the taunting to the gray bushy-tailed daredevils.

Mr. Beam, sensing his wife's enjoyment and talent with firearms, was suddenly afraid to joke around with the riflewoman. Then he had an idea. Mercenaries were called in. The grandsons all took part in the five-dollar-per-squirrel bounty. Zac, Gabe, Alex, and a couple of their friends each earned some spending money as the battle for the backyard finally began to turn for the Beams.

Mr. Beam called it the best money ever spent. The neighbors called it two weeks of horror as pellets flew through trees and into their yards. The war has subsided over the last few months. Mr. Beam still does not like squirrels, which makes it all the more fun to give him squirrel gifts. Squirrel salt and pepper shakers, squirrel dishes, squirrel nutcrackers—you get the idea—are all the rage at gatherings. By the way, Joey, if you are reading this, squirrel items are his favorite thing to receive if you are looking at a Father's Day present for him.

Mr. Beam's Daughter and the Strange Night Out

Author's note: There are many squirrel stories to tell, and the next one really happened. This was the last birthday that we would spend with my mom. She would leave this world just two months later. I am really glad our family got to share "one of those moments" as a memory of that evening.

Speaking of squirrelly times, this story surprisingly does not involve Mr. Beam but Mr. Beam's daughter, whom we will call Kathy, and the soon-to-be, once again, favorite son-in-law. My sister, Cindy, her husband, Mike, a friend of Mike's, Kathy, my mom, and I were all at dinner at a local restaurant that we will call Top of the River, celebrating Mom's birthday. Cindy and Mike were across from each other next to the wall of the long booth. My mom and the family friend were across from each other in the middle, and Kathy and I were across from each other on the aisle. Mom was suffering from a little dementia. She appeared to be having a good time even when the staff placed some crazy hat on her head and sang "Happy Birthday." Mom seemed to like the hat and continued to wear it throughout the dinner.

The other four at the table were talking or somewhat distracted when a gentleman (well, maybe that is not the correct term—a member of the male species) approached the table, looked at Kathy with a big smile, and said, "Lynn?" Kathy looked up, not saying anything, and he said, "Lynn, how are you—oh." He stopped midsentence as Kathy started to speak (but for one of the first times since I have known her, Kathy was speechless). He then said, "I'm sorry. I thought you was my first wife."

Well, this was just getting too good. I looked at the overzealous fellow with the brown T-shirt featuring a large black squirrel and bold lettering spelling out the words "Squirrel Whisperer." He had a smallish, thin frame that led you to believe he was capable of following the vermin into the tightest of spots. He would have to be the lead character for the show *Squirrel Dynasty,* if it is ever made. I wondered how in the world he ever caught a first wife, much less multiples, as he was implying.

I could not resist, so I stood up, acted shocked as I tossed my napkin on the table, and said, "Kathy, is there something that you did not tell me?"

The whisperer suddenly backpedaled and said, "No, no, this is not Lynn . . . I mean, I thought for a second you was her." He then looked toward Mom, as the whole table was now intrigued. He continued, "But I thought that lady was my ex-mother-in-law. Besides, she is much purtier than Lynn. I don't really like Lynn. I can't really stand her anymore, but I loved my mother-in-law and wanted to say hello to her. I am sorry to bother your dinner. I just thought it was them."

And just like that, the squirrel whisperer vanished. I suppose he vanished into a part of the county that I do not even know exists.

I glanced at Cindy and Mike, who were laughing hard, and Mom, with her hat on, just smiling as she finished her whole catfish. I looked at Kathy and started rolling with laughter. She returned my look with that "I am going to kill you" stare. I still occasionally joke and call her Lynn, and I am constantly on the lookout for another "squirrel whisperer." You never know when or where one might show up.

Mr. Beam—A Christmas Story

Author's note: I really do not know what to say about the "'Twas the Night" takeoff below. It was Christmas Eve, and I had shared many Mr. Beam stories on Facebook. A couple of folks sent me notes and asked if I could write a Mr. Beam story for Christmas, so I sat at the computer and wrote this in about ninety minutes. It just kind of flowed. Some of the comments from friends at the end of the post were very kind. The funniest thing about this is that I posted it a couple of hours before Joey had decided to make a post, a post talking about the favorite son-in-law and some family reunion meetings that he had attended and I had not. His writing was also to the "'Twas the Night" poem, and after he saw mine, he could not make his post. He did read it to us the next day at the Beams. It was funny and certainly a humorous poke at me. I was lucky and glad that I had beaten him to the draw. Timing is everything!

'Twas the night before Christmas, and all is well, it would
seem
But something still troubled the curious Mr. Beam.
Yes, the house was in order and the lawn cut just right,
For the gathering family that would come at first light.
After a busy day, Mrs. Beam had made it to bed,
Dreaming of Hawaii and a lei around her head.
Mr. Beam, with his broom, swept a speck off the floor,

Then straightened the wreath he had hung on the door.
When out on the lawn, there arose such a clatter,
That he opened the door to see what was the matter.
Away to the backyard, he moved at limited speed,
'Til his bare toes landed in a pile of birdseed.
The moon up above gave the Earth some bright light,
And Mr. Beam saw that things were just not quite right.
What to his wondering eyes did appear,
Pieces of birdhouses scattered far away and some near.
He had carefully placed them on strong limbs in the trees,
So the grandkids could watch pretty birds if you please.
Suddenly, he felt like he had been hit with a brick,
His knees got wobbly, and he felt a bit sick.
Then his sickness turned to anger as he figured things out,
And his face glowed bright red, and he started to pout.
"Squirrels, squirrels," he yelled in the night,
"Gray, brown, or black, you are in for a fight."
The battle with the vermin had gone on for years,
But the assault on Christmas Eve almost brought him to
tears.
His beautiful backyard, a sanctuary for birds,
Could now not be described with any kind words.
And then, with a twinkling, he heard on the roof,
Turning, he saw several squirrels all aloof.
He went to his shed to pull out his ladder,
Climbed a few rungs and saw the squirrels scatter.
Frustrated, he stood a few feet off the ground,
When he looked up above, he heard a strange sound.
"Ho! Ho! Ho!" rang out from the night sky.
"Goodness," said Mr. Beam, "I forgot about that guy."
Methodically down the ladder and in the house he did creep,
Slipped under the covers and pretended to sleep.
It was just a few moments, and he began to snore;

Sunshine and Mrs. Beam's urging made his feet hit the floor.
"Come quick! Hurry, Jerry! Oh, this you must see!"
The backyard was glistening with decor on each tree.
Birdhouses in place and all in one piece,
Birds were everywhere; there were even two geese.
Orioles, robins, two turtledoves, and a jay,
Had come to Mr. Beams to enjoy Christmas Day.
The elf in the sky, St. Nick he is called,
Had spruced and straightened for Mr. Beam and all.
The families arrived and were all in good cheer,
But Mr. Beam had a bad sense that a squirrel might be near.
All gifts were exchanged except one behind a chair;
It was for Mr. Beam, a mystery gift from somewhere.
He opened with caution, joked, and had fun,
Then laughed with delight at his new pellet gun.
St. Nick had made him ready for the squirrels to slay,
As he said, "Merry Christmas to all, and to all a good day!"

Forty Years Between Flights

Authors note: Kathy and I have had the good fortune to travel to a few fun places. We had some memorable vacations with Gabe and Alex, but we had not been anywhere with Mr. and Mrs. Beam for quite some time. Joey, Karen, and Zac have had the Beams' company on several excursions, and I knew I needed to catch up. My dad had served on the Alabama Housing Finance Authority Board from its inception in the early 1980s until his death in 2012. The state senator from our district, Clay Scofield, had the governor's authority for the next appointment to the board. He asked if I would take my dad's place. I was honored. The annual meeting of housing boards from across the nation chose Portsmouth, New Hampshire, for the 2013 site. Kathy and I convinced the Beams to take the journey with us by telling them we would check out Maine as well. The next few stories are from that trip. Another story from the Hawaii trip references a traveling incident from the return flight home from Maine. You will need to wait until Hawaii for that tale.

As Kathy and I discussed the idea of Mr. and Mrs. Beam traveling with us up the East Coast, we were both concerned about how they would handle the flight and the bustling airports. When they agreed to go with us, we began to try to simplify the process for them. We decided to fly from Birmingham to Boston. Although neither had been on a commercial air flight since the 1970s, they remained calm and relaxed throughout the experience. It turned out to be a great day to fly. The sunny sky gave us great views of the Atlantic coastline, including a spectacular view of the New York City skyline from thirty-five thousand feet. Their seats were directly behind ours. I got a little cracked up at the amount of giggling and the smiles from the two of them. I remained a little uptight for all of us, as I was preparing, in my mind, the best route to leave Logan International Airport in Boston to head up to New Hampshire.

I am not a fan of driving in Boston. I must admit that the town once again got the best of me. I missed the quick first turn heading into the tunnel that I had wanted to take to get downtown in order to visit the Old North Church and grab some lunch. After finding a place to turn around, I once again attempted an advance on the historic city. Well, downtown was blocked due to a festival happening, and barricades were everywhere. I got lost several times and seemed to be circling the city, weaving in and out of pedestrians and roadblocks. The Beams, much like they were in the airplane, seemed unfazed. I actually wondered what tranquilizer they had consumed before leaving Albertville. It almost reminded me of the Chevy Chase and Goldie Hawn movie *Foul Play*, and the Beams were the Japanese couple in the back of the limo laughing and believing they were in a scene from *Kojak* as the car swerved recklessly through the streets of San Francisco. Finally, with nowhere to park and my nerves a little worn, I decided that we would forego the Boston adventure and head on up to Portsmouth.

I had no idea that once you escaped the clutches of downtown and headed north on I-95, there was not much to this part of the world. I might as well have been driving through parts of Montana. With our stomachs growling, we finally found a place that reminded me of the old Albertville Family restaurant in our hometown from back in the day. It was a white block building with a few Harleys out front, so we knew it was probably pretty good eating. Having traveled a few places, I tried just to nod and not say a whole lot when I walked in. But not Mr. Beam—no, he just blurted out to the hostess, "Where is your men's room?"

The place got quiet, and the bearded bikers looked up and over at the four of us. The lady asked him to repeat the question in her northeast Boston (Bahstan) accent. Again, Mr. Beam asked for directions to the men's room. The smiling hostess once again asked him to repeat it, but I personally think it was for entertainment purposes. She wanted her regular patrons to be able to hear Mr. Beam talk again. She politely showed him the way and said something like, "You must be from Mississippi or somewhere."

Aaaagghhh, I thought. Being from Alabama, the two states you do not want to be confused about being from are Mississippi and Kentucky. Those are whole different levels of Southern. We chose to go with sandwiches and make a fast meal of it. When Mr. Beam ordered a grilled cheese with extra cheese and grape jelly on the side, I thought the waitress was going to bust a gut laughing. We were careful ordering iced tea, as we remembered the story of the favorite son-in-law, before his preaching days, being served an Asti Spumante when the waiter could not understand the dialect and misunderstood "iced tea" for "Asti." That event also took place in the state of Massachusetts.

As we exited the restaurant, the various voices of our new friends could be heard all the way in the parking lot saying things like, "Y'all come back real soon" and "Next time we will have sweet tea for y'all," along with some roaring laughter. I looked at Kathy and said, "I suppose we made their day. No telling what stories will be told about us this evening."

A Mr. Beamism is one of those comments that you cannot help but remember. He has a number of them, and they spring out of him at any given time. A Beamism occurred as we were approaching the Atlantic coastline, and we began to see views of the water. As Mr. Beam observed the brown area from the tree line to the water in some places, he said, "They sure could use some rain. Look how low the water is."

"Mr. Beam," I responded, trying not to sound like a smart-aleck son-in-law, "that is the ocean, and I believe it is just low tide. It should fill up nicely in a few hours."

Bless him, Lord, I thought to myself as I stole a line from many of a Missionary Baptist Church testimony service. If you can't say anything else about traveling with Mr. Beam, at least it is always entertaining.

Mr. Beam, Water Walker

Speaking of low tides, I suppose the reason they named Bar Harbor, Maine, what they did is due to the lengthy, almost mystical strip of land that surfaces during low tide and connects the town from Bridge Street to Bar Island. Bar Island is not large but is included as part of Acadia National Park. Many attempts have been made by the leadership of Bar Harbor over the last century to include Bar Island as part of their domain. But it appears in 1798, the town of Gouldsboro, Maine, claimed the island in its articles of incorporation. Gouldsboro and Bar Harbor are only ten miles apart as the seagull flies over the ocean, but over thirty-seven miles apart by road. Logic would dictate that a three-quarter-mile sandbar connection would be deemed a bit more conducive for management, but I digress and delve into politics, an area where logic so many times fails to find its way into the people in control of such things . . .

Sorry, I can't let it go. I mean, when is the last time someone from Gouldsboro has walked across a sandbar to Bar Island? Not recently, I should say. Even from Bar Harbor, the window of time to access the island is limited. The sandbar begins to appear about ninety minutes before low tide and that same ninety-minute window as the tide begins to rise once again.

There is risk in any adventure, but I have quickly learned the risks exponentially increase when Mr. Beam is involved. These risks are not necessarily injury-related for the mild-mannered man but perils of things like getting lost, talking in his Southern accent to strangers, stepping into a fox's den, or needing to find a bathroom. The Bar Island adventure has one major warning: "Make sure you leave the island before the high tide." If you do not make it on time, you basically have a strong possibility of spending the night on Bar Island or swimming the almost-one-mile distance in the northern Atlantic's frigid waters. There is a little wildlife on the island, but nothing that should be life-threatening if kept at a cautious distance.

When we strolled toward the harbor, we noticed that the sandbar was fully visible. People were now walking, kayaking, and even driving toward Bar Island. We decided to give it a try. We walked. There was no way I was going to drive a rental car across a sandbar, especially when I did not know our timing. Were we in the middle of low tide, or was the water on the rise again? We joined the migration, and after a few stops to look at shells, tidal pools, and small creatures of the Atlantic, we found ourselves at the beginning of a trail leading to the top of Bar Island. As we ascended the well-worn dirt path through the evergreen trees, I kept one vigilant eye on the dirt bridge leading back to town and the other on the lookout for mushrooms to photograph. My obsession with the growing fungi is literally a story for another day. At one point, the trail split, and so did we—Kathy and I heading upward, and Mr. and Mrs. Beam in another direction.

As we cleared the tree line, we beheld purple-flowered meadows, a couple of passing deer, a tree so large that it would make the Clark Griswold family smile at Christmas, some bricks, and remains of a fireplace. Our minds thought of a time past when someone either lived or had a vacation home on the island. The 360-degree view from that spot had magnificent sights of the ocean, the town of Bar Harbor, and the small landmass known as Sheep Porcupine Island. We took photos and enjoyed the moment and then headed back to the trailhead. Mr. Beam and Mrs. Beam were there. Mr. Beam was talking to some fellow septuagenarians who were entering their kayaks to make it across the harbor. I looked and realized that the sandbar had seriously decreased in size, and there were no more cars on our side.

It is a recurring theme that when Mr. Beam is involved, he may not be the swiftest of sprinters in a hundred-meter dash. As a matter of fact, one might consider his gait when walking to be turtlesque. Mrs. Beam doesn't normally say a whole lot, but words that she constantly uses when they are strolling are, "Hurry up, Jerry," "Come on Jerry," or "Jerry, they are waiting on you." Mr. Beam attributes his lack of speed to a knee injury he obtained as a young man when he fell off a tractor. He is quick to pull up his trouser leg to show you the scar and is not shy about letting everyone know that the injury is the reason he did not make it to the NFL. He usually meanders seventy to eighty yards behind the rest of us.

We decided the time had come to make our move back across the sandbar. Mrs. Beam, Kathy, and I began our normal pace, and soon Mr. Beam was falling behind. About midway and also the lowest elevation of the sandbar, I heard Mr. Beam say, "Go ahead, I'll be fine." I turned to see him laughing as the ocean crept ever closer to him. So many things raced through my mind as I looked at him. *Should I go after him? His feet are about to get wet. I hope his friend in the kayak is close by if needed.* The weirdest was the surreal moment when I thought of the Exodus as Moses led the Israelites on dry ground across the Red Sea and then Pharaoh's army being washed away. Mr. Beam's fate was looking like that of one of the soldiers. Somehow, maybe by divine intervention, he made it. Maybe it was due to the extra narrow shoes that protect his feet, but he did get to town.

As we discussed things while eating ice cream on the grassy knoll overlooking the harbor, a couple of young boys with plastic swords waged an epic swashbuckling battle, reminding me of Gabe and Alex twenty years earlier. It is funny how the mind wanders in moments like that, for then my mind raced to Bob Seger's song "Like a Rock" and the well-written lyrics "Twenty years now, where'd they go? Twenty years, I don't know. I sit and I wonder sometimes, where they've gone." As the duel continued, two young ladies sporting black, above-the-knee dresses with black boots appeared and walked toward the gazebo. They had cameras and were setting up shots with the perfect background setting. One had middle-of-the-back-length pink hair that reminded me of a 1980s Cyndi Lauper video. The other had hair that was short in the back, but the front featured two long portions that ended below her waist. Aquamarine is the best way that I know to describe the color. The girls caught the attention of Mr. Beam. He asked me to see if he could get a picture made with the ladies. I thought the girls might think it a little creepy for me to make such a request, but I assured Mr. Beam that if he made the request, I would take the pictures. A few moments later, Mr. Beam had his arm around the two young ladies with the rocker look in a gazebo at Bar Harbor while his for-the-moment-favorite son-in-law took photographs commemorating the occasion. Mrs. Beam and Kathy just watched and shook their heads.

As we settled back on the fire-ant-free grass, I mentioned my thoughts and the Red Sea comparison from our earlier hike. Mr. Beam quickly pointed out that it was not the Red Sea but the Sea of Galilee and a New Testament story that should have been the comparison. I know Mr. Beam to be a strong man of faith and a firm believer in Jesus, but I quickly excused myself and took up another view of the harbor a safe distance away in case of a sudden bolt of lightning.

Mr. Beam, Tomb Raider

I really like Bar Harbor, Maine. I like the way the town runs alongside the ocean with just enough of an inlet to protect the boats. I love Acadia National Park, which is minutes away. The downtown has a Gatlinburg, Tennessee, feel, with restaurants and shops containing ice cream, candy, souvenirs, clothes, and all sorts of artwork. During this stay, I enjoyed the three-block strolls back and forth from our flower-garden-decorated bed and breakfast to the main area of commerce. I enjoyed walking past the churches and even the cemeteries. There is just something extra spooky about the New England graveyards. The wrought-iron fence around one in particular had a large gate. The fence had posts close enough and high enough to keep the dogs and large animals at bay. Of course, the squirrels and black cats could find a way in, which added to the mysterious ambiance when you caught them out of the corner of your eye and thought, *What was that?* while trying to laugh it off.

As you forced the gate open, rusty hinges seemed to cry out in a painful way before moving just enough to let one person at a time pass. The centuries-old trees that border this cemetery have large branches that block out the sun and reach for you like the ghost of the past in a Dickens tale. As you make your way from grave marker to grave marker, there is something different. Maybe it is the fact that so many of their dead left this world in the 1700s, or maybe it is just that cool breeze off the ocean that tickles the back of your neck, but something sets them apart. I avoided the midnight strolls. The ones around dusk had my mind racing with all sorts of childhood tales of the terrifying characters Bloody Bones and Scary Eyes. I imagined the time that the townsfolk were living and how harsh the elements must have been in that area, especially in the winter. It was almost as if they wanted to share their story as you viewed their birth and departure dates. Some left this world seemingly way too young.

The meticulous Mr. Beam could not pass the area without stopping to pick up a few limbs that had fallen around the departed or bending over to pull some stray weeds attempting to make their way from the concrete sidewalks to the sky. He picked up rocks and any and everything he thought gave the place an unkempt look. I was just hoping he did not pick up some old sailor's medallion with something like the "Curse of the Black Pearl" accompanying the bearer. He would say something about how these cemeteries sure would look better with some fresh flowers on the graves and that they need to have a Decoration Sunday in Bar Harbor.

Now, I must confess that there is some irony here. The fact is, I am not really a graveyard-type guy. I do enjoy some of the historic sites. I thought that Burial Hill in Plymouth, Massachusetts, with the grave of William Bradford, was pretty neat. I have visited Arlington and Pearl Harbor. Both moved me in a special way. The realization of the sacrifices made for our freedom and the reverence shown at these sites are some things that you do not forget. However, in the South, one celebration that I do not understand is decoration. Family reunions, church socials, and picnics in the cemetery during the month of May just seem weird. This is another reason that I fall behind Pastor Joey as the favorite son-in-law. The Beams are all about the tradition of decorations.

Joey, the daughter we will call Karen, and good ole Zac show up for all the events. Due to my corruption of the daughter we will call Kathy, she has not attended a decoration in thirty years. Shoot, Mr.

Beam is so into decorations that the day before the event, he will load his lawn mower in the back of his bright-blue truck and make sure that the grass on the graves of the loved ones is no more than an inch and a half high. Most of the time, the cemetery keepers have already been working to make the place look good. Sometimes, the keepers of the grave do not appreciate the competition and tedious attention to detail that Mr. Beam puts into his work. One groundskeeper got so angry that he threatened to call the police and throw Mr. Beam off the premises. Mr. Beam could hardly contain his laughter during the discussion, which only infuriated the keeper more. As the threats became almost physical, Annie Oakley (Mrs. Beam) stepped between the two, giving the cemetery worker a rarely seen or heard tongue-lashing. That seemed to end the issue, at least for the time. Mr. Beam, frustrated that the site was not groomed to his liking, did leave. He returned well after dark and completed the task of beautifying the family graves under the high-beam lights of the truck.

My lack of attending decorations is only a part of the problem. You see, Mr. and Mrs. Beam have already purchased and placed headstones at the site of their future resting place. People tell me how nice they look, although I have not personally seen them. I think it is a bit disconcerting to have your name and date of birth already inscribed and waiting on the ending date, but maybe that is just me. Even Jesus did not have his own tomb but was placed in the tomb of Joseph of Arimathea. Of course, Jesus only borrowed the tomb for a very short time and is no longer there. Amen! That is another thing about the gravesites: I believe that my loved ones have already taken off from there and are enjoying the afterlife. I mean, I get it. I understand that it is a place to reflect and remember. I just feel that I can do that anywhere, but to each his own.

The kicker is that the Beams have memorial vases for flowers on their sites. Mr. Beam—the man who grows beautiful flowers in his squirrel-infested yard, the man who cuts the flowers and places them in beautiful arrangements and takes them to people, brightening their day—seems to have one simple request: "Will someone bring me flowers after I am gone?" I was not trying to be mean when I told him he might need to rethink that vase thing. I just told him that an empty vase might look, well, sad. He reminds me that he sure is glad Joey is around. He is just so sure that Joey will make sure things look good. Joey, Joey, Joey, aye yi yi—it is certainly hard to compete with the perfect pastor brother-in-law.

Mr. Beam Goes to Hawaii!

Author's note: It finally happened. The timing was right for Kathy and me to ask her parents to join us for a trip to the islands. We had made four previous trips and knew which islands we enjoyed the most. It would be the first trip for the Beams. The trip was one of those that almost did not happen. Mr. Beam was diagnosed with shingles about three weeks before we were scheduled to leave. He was also feeling very weak, but he looked at Mrs. Beam when she asked him for the last time if he could make the trip. "Yes, Jane"—one of his pet names for Martha—"I want to go."

When it comes to visiting Hawaii, everyone has their "must-see" places. We decided we would visit Maui, Lanai, and Kauai on our ten-day vacation. Omitting Oahu was hard to do. Mr. Beam would have loved Pearl Harbor. Mrs. Beam would have enjoyed Diamond Head, and they both would have shopped at the International Market Place. We felt that we may truly only have one shot to share with them the areas that we have found to be the most beautiful—and so in May of 2014, off we went. We would spend Kathy's birthday, May 4th (aka Star Wars Day), and Mother's Day away. The Hawaii stories are in order, and the first story was also the first Mr. Beam story to hit Facebook. The original story was short and to the point as I described a scene. The comments from the readers were overwhelmingly positive, so I tried another and then another. By the time we got back, Mr. Beam had hit rock-star status in our small town. For the book, I added information to the first story to help describe the day.

Mr. Beam and the Bird!

Traveling by plane with today's security concerns and the "fill every seat" mentality of profit-driven carriers is a challenge for passengers of all ages. To top it off, the Beams were traveling with one of those "we gotta be there early for everything" people—me. We had decided to take the first flight from Birmingham to Dallas. The plane left at 6:30 a.m. We would need to leave Albertville at 4:00 a.m. to make it to the airport by 5:30 a.m. Up at 3:00 a.m., Kathy and I made our way to Howard Avenue. The Beams were ready and waiting. We got to the airport ahead of schedule, and I was feeling pretty good about the start of the trip. The just-over-two-hour flight to Dallas was uneventful.

Arriving in Dallas, we had just enough time to find the gate and try to buy some food for the seven-hour direct flight to Maui. It blows my mind that they no longer feed you on such trips unless you are willing to pay high prices with your credit card only. Again, other than a long flight, everything went smoothly. I had called ahead and arranged for a taxi to pick us up. Like clockwork, we were greeted and began the forty-minute ride to Wailea on the southwest part of the island.

Another great thing about taking the first flight out is that you can steal an afternoon. Due to the five hours that we gained soaring through the time zones, we were at the hotel by around 2:30 p.m. local time. We placed our bags with the bellmen and headed toward the pool with the outdoor grill for some food. It was equivalent to 7:30 p.m. in Alabama, and we were famished. The beauty of the hotel grounds, pool, and the ocean in the background began to set the peaceful tone that we would enjoy for the next few days.

As you have probably witnessed at many outdoor restaurants, birds are always around. This day, the bird world apparently had spread the word that the man with the amazing backyard and love for feathered friends was now sitting at this table. They were everywhere, surrounding us, first a few feet away, and as the food arrived, ever closer. They seemed to know that the afternoon large burgers were engulfed with huge buns and the opportunity for many crumbs.

Mrs. Beam, Kathy, and I dug in after the food was blessed. We listened as Mr. Beam talked about the flowers as he methodically prepared his food for the first taste. I sensed a little disappointment as he realized that there were no syrup or guava jelly condiments to sweeten up the grain-fed beef burger. Mr. Beam, as he is prone to do, was talking while he pinched off a bite to eat. He used his hand to tell the story and kind of waved the food in the air. One bird took this as a goodwill gesture and started to fly toward the morsel as Mr. Beam brought it to his mouth. Mr. Beam never saw it coming. From my point of view, it looked like the bird almost went totally inside his mouth, with maybe the right wing and the tail feathers just outside the cavernous orifice. The echo of the victorious chirp sounded at the exact moment the winged bandit snatched the food from Mr. Beam's fingers, causing him to chomp on nothing but air. Flying speedily away to a safe landing spot, this bird had garnered the respect and admiration of all the other birds for its fearless act. They flew to his side to congratulate him or maybe to share in the spoils. Before we left the table, our hunger pangs had been settled. Mr. Beam was now the birdman of Wailea, and we all had a moment to remember. If only my camera could have caught the action and the expressions—can't make this stuff up.

Mr. Beam and the Phrase "That'll Be Fine"

We all know how Mr. Beam does not want to be any trouble for anyone, and whatever anybody else wants to do is okay with him. Although it is certainly a compatible attitude, it can be a bit confusing when you have accent barriers and everyone wants to please everybody else. There is an old *Seinfeld* episode about low-talkers. It refers to people who talk so softly that you cannot hear them. Mr. Beam's daughter, whom we will call Kathy, does not have this problem, and Mr. Beam does not in normal conversation, but just place a menu around him and seat him at a table, and he makes the dog whisperer sound like Don Rickles.

Case 1: At breakfast yesterday, Mr. Beam ordered the special, which does not include meat. As he ordered, the waiter asked if he indeed wanted bacon with that. Mr. Beam said, "That'll be fine," as he was talking to me. The waiter leaned his ear a little closer as if he needed Mr. Beam to clarify, which he did not. Breakfast came, and a generous plate of bacon was placed at the center of the table. As the meal progressed, Kathy asked him why he was not eating his bacon. His response was that he did not order any bacon, at which point we all assured him that he had. Needless to say, we watched in amazement as Mr. Beam polished off the big platter of bacon.

Case 2: After dinner one night, the French waiter asked us about dessert. He mentioned that bread pudding was included with the meal. Kathy, Mrs. Beam, and I were too full. He then mentioned that he could prepare it to go, at which point Mr. Beam said that he would like one to go. I was sitting directly across from the man, and I could barely hear him.

The waiter said, "One or four to go?"

At which point, Mr. Beam said, "That'll be fine."

The waiter came out with a grocery sack heavy enough to hide under during a tornado, which had four bread puddings. We said thanks and made Mr. Beam carry it (until he got tired and made Mrs. Beam lug it around awhile). We then decided to walk around the beautiful outdoor mall. Mr. Beam, being the kind soul that he is and becoming a bit weary of carrying the dessert around, decided he would attempt to share his food with others. Aye, yi yi, it was all a bit embarrassing. I had to get away, so I went to the upstairs area and watched from above as one of the grandfathers of my children began to approach vacationers and islanders alike, attempting to coerce them into taking a bread pudding. Alas, there were no takers. Watching it unfold reminded me of the days of old when someone would approach you at an airport, give you a flower, and stand there waiting for a tip of some kind. But Mr. Beam wanted no tip. He was just trying to be nice.

As he went from store to store, back and forth across the mall, my mind drifted to the days of Atari and the game Pong. Mr. Beam was being sent slowly back and forth by the rejection of the paddles and failing to score. Finally, finally, a young culinary student took him up on the offer. Sensing some momentum and rejuvenation from a slightly lighter bag, he tried his best to give one to the custodian, who stood there leaning on his broom, shaking his head. As Mr. Beam walked away, the custodian began sweeping and said to the culinary student, "I did not understand a word he said."

To say he made friends might be an overstatement. To say he had people calling the authorities to see if any loonies were on the loose might be more accurate. He left the mall with three bread puddings and decided he would eat them for breakfast the next morning. Morning came, and the bread pudding had cooled. Mr. Beam tried but did not even eat the first of them. He was disappointed that he had not enjoyed one the night before and that he had wasted the good dessert. We finally had to tell him not to worry, "that it will be fine."

Mr. Beam's Daughter and the Fancy Boutiques

Mr. Beam, as many of you know, has two daughters. One whom we will call Karen is married to a wonderful man serving as pastor of a thriving Baptist church. He is generally deemed as the favorite son-in-law. His other daughter, let's call her Kathy, is married to . . . well, me (bless her, Lord, as Mr. Beam would say). This story is more about Mr. Beam's daughter, Kathy, and Mrs. Beam. These two ladies were shopping at the Shops of Wailea. Yes, this is the same mall area of the now-famous "bread-pudding peddler," as the local newspaper called the curious man with a sometimes barely audible Southern accent. It was, in fact, the very next evening, and it is fair to say that even though Mr. Beam made the trek with the rest of us, Mrs. Beam had him under very close surveillance. She was not the only one, it seemed; everywhere we went that evening, the mall security strolled by.

But wait, this is not a Mr. Beam story. This is a story about the daughter we will call Kathy. It is hard to write about Kathy without a shopping environment, so here we are, back at the mall. This outdoor mall has many stores, but some are fairly upscale. There is a Tiffany's, Rolex, Coach, and Louis Vuitton (which I would have never guessed was spelled with an *I* in it), to name a few. Kathy and Mrs. Beam were not necessarily in those stores, but it is safe to say that many of the shoppers in that area frequent such places. Kathy, as usual, was looking good! She was sporting a light-turquoise/blue dress with some darker stripes—quite sharp, you might say. During her shopping experience, two different ladies came up and bragged about her dress and wanted to know which of the chic stores had offered such fabulous, tasteful attire. Kathy was gracious as they went on about the dress, assuring them that she had not purchased it in Maui but at one of the Alabama boutiques. They went away disappointed, figuring they would not make it to Alabama to shop. As we were leaving, Kathy commented that she did not have the heart to tell the impressively jeweled women that they could buy the beautiful outfit at their local Wal-Mart store—then again, they will probably never know.

Authors note: The three previous stories were posted on Facebook, one for each day we were on Maui. It would be unjust not to mention why we love Wailea. First, this particular area has the convenience of Wailea Tennis Center. Kathy and I are avid tennis players and play each day we stay there. It is a short walk from the Marriott. Second, the aforementioned shops are right beside the hotel, featuring many fine restaurants as well as a great place to people-watch. Third is the amazing concrete walking path that allows for miles of easy strolls or exerting runs along the beach while enjoying the picturesque ocean views. Fourth are the sunsets. I will take a moment and try to describe them in the next story.

Mr. Beam and the Glimpse of Heaven

Infinity pools are captivating and can be spectacular. The one at the Marriott Wailea is both. It is also for adults only (we had to take a family vote on whether Mr. Beam could join us there; the vote was two to one, with Mrs. Beam abstaining). Inside the pool, it appears you could swim to Bora Bora, as the water seems to continue into the ocean and go on and on. The color of the water appears to blend as the bright rich blues stretch until they meet the lighter blue of the sky. The lawn and deck chairs from behind the pool face the ocean and the walking path. The well-manicured, dark-green grass areas contrast beautifully with the rich, black lava rock. The black surface is wet from the white foam spray of the ocean waves intermittently splashing high into the air.

We took our seats at about 5:15 p.m., only minutes before the area became standing room only. The guests were enjoying themselves. The waitresses from the grill were taking orders for food and drinks. Some adults splashed while others held each other like newlyweds in the pool. Straight beyond the pool, the bright yellow sun was making its way down. The last intense rays of heat that had provided the mid-eighties temperatures for the day added that one more layer of pink to the fair-skinned guests. Sunglasses were covering every eye as the bright light also reflected off the water while dropping nearer to the sea. On the right side of the setting sun was the island of Lanai. To the left was the island of Kahoolawe, a tiny island even smaller; but at six miles from Maui, it is two miles closer than Lanai.

As you looked toward Kahoolawe, just beyond the walking path was a single monkeypod tree creating shade for the oceanside grassy knoll around it. This evening, chairs were in two sections, and people were standing around preparing for a sunset wedding. A couple of boys were in their dress shirts and slacks, complete with matching vests, and barefoot as they wrestled around, adding a touch of grass stain to the wardrobe. It was, however, the two flower girls who made the four of us smile. They were dressed alike in what appeared to be a beige leotard-type outfit with white skirts made of chiffon, which flowed behind them as they laughed and ran, also shoeless, around the grounds. Their long blonde hair had been curled for the evening and was held in place by headbands and a bow. The whole scene was fabulous.

Suddenly, there was a bright flash of yellow light as the sun seemed to touch the water. Sighs were heard from the people watching as all heads turned toward the west to see what would happen next. Then there was silence, not a word or a splash, not a slurp or a smack, just silence. What was happening before our very eyes mesmerized everyone around the pool and on the grounds. Sunglasses were raised to the top of heads as the strong, dark silhouettes of Lanai and Kahoolawe contrasted with the brilliant light show between the two landmasses. The bright-blue water kissed the vibrant orange, crimson, pink, red, yellow, and lavender colors left by the setting sun at the very moment the groom kissed the bride on the grassy knoll under the silhouette of the lone tree. Still, there was silence, reverent silence as God, the Master Artist, concluded His masterpiece. We felt we had witnessed our Creator painting a picture just for us.

Suddenly, applause was heard from our left as the bride and groom were introduced and the wedding party began to leave. The two flower girls then ran along the pathway toward the infinity pool, giggling and laughing as they made their way. Their headbands created the look of a halo as their hair flowed in the breeze. The skirts sweeping behind them gave the appearance of wings. As they ran in front of the sunset, their shadows became the likeness of angels, and their laughter a soothing tonic. It was truly magical. Mr. Beam understood why Kathy and I enjoyed coming to Maui for moments like this—things you just cannot explain unless you see it. As a believer, I felt God was showing us a little bit of what heaven will be like, only more beautiful. After all, it was only a glimpse.

Author's note: We left Maui, choosing to take the ferry to Lanai. It is about a forty-minute ride, and during certain months of the year, whales can be seen in the channel. In May, we were a bit late to see them, but we scanned the deep blue waters just in case. Maui is quite diverse with its landscape. From the Haleakala Crater to the sea, you pass by everything from deserts to farms to rain forest. But for us, it is those sunsets to the west that set it apart.

Lanai is a totally different island. Formerly known for growing pineapples and owned by the Dole family, it is now a limited vacation destination. It boasts an older hotel in downtown Lanai City (population about two thousand) and two Four Seasons Resorts. They are quite nice. One is located on the beach, and the other is a lodge in the mountains. The temperatures at the beach are typical Hawaii, maybe a touch warmer in the mid-eighties; at the Lodge, they will range between sixty and seventy-two degrees. Also at the Lodge, fires are built in the evenings in the grand gathering room near the restaurant. It is a totally unique Hawaiian experience. If you stay at one of the Four Seasons, you get the benefits of both, complete with a shuttle that runs between the two locations on the half hour. If Maui is the sunset and one of the adventure islands, then Lanai is the relaxation island. So, the next group of stories take place on Lanai.

Mr. Beam and the Orchid House

If you know Mr. Beam at all, then you realize he has a passion for beautiful flowers and shrubs, as well as a total dislike of squirrels. Well, this story has nothing to do with the latter and everything to do with the former.

Upon our arrival at the public loading dock on Lanai, we were met by the shuttle bus that would take us on the nine-mile trip to the Lodge at Koele, one of the two Four Seasons Resorts on the island. We were greeted on the sprawling front porch with a hug, lei, hot towel, and a cool island juice to help us unwind from the journey. Lush foliage abounds in the many beautiful garden areas at the Lodge. Kathy and I had visited before and wanted to quickly see Mr. Beam's reaction to the grounds. We entered the front door and proceeded through the grand hall, out the back doors, and on to the walking path that traversed the massive pond filled with koi and the surrounding acreage. Things like elephant ears that are as big as—well, elephant ears—and a manicured dark-green lawn provide gorgeous backgrounds to many flowers, including my personal favorite, the hibiscus. They come in many vibrant colors, including one the color of a Maui sunset.

We began our stroll around the grounds with the Beams. There were concrete paths meandering in and around the gardens. On the west side of the pond were huge dark-green bushes filled with vibrant pink, coral, and purple flowers. I was going to show off my horticulture knowledge while hoping to make some points with the father-in-law and mentioned that I had never seen such beautiful azaleas. Mr. Beam shook his head, and with that look that said, "Kathy, how could you ever marry someone this dumb?", he quickly corrected, "I believe those are begonias, but they are beautiful." Rats, I had blown it again.

We stayed on the path past the lawn putt-putt course and around the meditation area. Before long, we saw a large greenhouse-looking structure next to one of the paths and walked over to see what it might offer. "Orchid House" was printed on the sign. We went in to see orchids of many shapes and colors, appearing to the untrained observer to be healthy and ready to be utilized wherever the need might arise in and around the Lodge. But the professional landscaper eye of Mr. Beam saw something different, possibly threatening. He spoke out and mentioned that the orchids looked dry and needed water. He started walking around the house, searching as he went for a water bucket or garden hose.

Kathy and I, a bit concerned, glanced at each other as Mrs. Beam said, "Now, Jerry, they don't need your help." We chimed in, mentioning how good everything else looked around the resort and quickly tried to come up with a way to get Mr. Beam out of there before he watered every plant in the orchid house.

A couple of days later, as Kathy and I strolled the grounds, we noticed a gardener at the orchid house with a bucket of sand working hard to replant many species of orchids. We stopped to see what was up. He said something to the effect that the leaves of the orchids were turning yellow, and it appeared they had been overwatered. He was sure he had followed his normal routine. Kathy and I had our suspicions about the gardener's little helper, but we never asked. We were quite sure we did not want to know the truth—the truth that the ever-helpful Mr. Beam had somehow snuck away that fateful first evening and helped himself to the water hose just outside the orchid house.

Mr. Beam and the Resting Place

Now, this story is not an eyewitness account. I was not there. However, it is rapidly becoming local Hawaiian folklore, and I am sure will be passed down for generations on the islands. Mr. and Mrs. Beam had been strolling the grounds for a while when Mr. Beam spotted a place to rest close to the pool. The hammock was securely tied between two very sturdy trees. Thinking that he might get an hour's nap, Mr. Beam climbed in the middle and was immediately engulfed by the netting as the hammock settled ever so close to the ground. Suddenly, the relaxation spot became a battleground (Mr. Beam wanting out, and the hammock acting like a Venus flytrap wanting to keep him for a while). Finally, he struggled his hands free of the netting but could not roll out of the hammock because it was so close to the ground. He could not get his feet extended to get out. Mrs. Beam could not hear the pleas for help, so he was on his own.

Eventually, with one courageous push, he lunged upward, heaving his body from the strong hold of the interwoven, overgrown ball of twine, as he would later call it. The effort sent him flopping out of the hammock to the solid ground into yet another dilemma. The solid ground was sloped, and Mr. Beam was now careening toward the crystal-blue swimming pool. Extending his legs straight out, he slowed the gravitational force enough to keep from being the only fully clothed swimmer at the Lodge. As he began to stand, and as his head was still spinning, he decided to try and walk, landing one foot into the step area of the pool. For the next forty minutes or so, he collected many stares, and snickering was heard as the squishing sound of his shoe let everyone know that Mr. Beam was very close by.

Mr. Beam and the Booster Shot

Many of you (Facebook followers) may not know that on Easter Sunday, less than two weeks before our trip, Mr. Beam was battling a case of shingles and fatigue. It was not certain that the Beams would make the trip until about three or four days before when he began to feel better and was determined to make the trek. The doctors, along with other medications, had been giving him booster shots and had sent one to take on the trip.

The trip started great for Mr. Beam. He seemed energetic and ready to take on the world—but by the time he found himself in a sand trap on a putt-putt course and taking two shots to get out of it, you could see it change. The lefty made the par-51, grass course look like Augusta National as he ballooned to a 17-over-par 68, eleven strokes behind the cross-hand-putting Mrs. Beam. It was time for the booster shot, but who was going to inject Mr. Beam?

For some reason, everyone (except for me) had a crystal-clear memory of me giving allergy shots to myself thirty years ago. That, coupled with a sister who is a nurse practitioner and my countless hours treating cramps and sprains as the Aggie tennis coach, made me the guy. We gathered on the deck of their Koele Lodge room, and the syringe was pulled out. Mr. Beam seemed to remember the doctor saying that everything would be ready; just open the package and stick it in. Now, being a tennis coach, I had seen an EpiPen and knew about the simple injection system of use in the case of someone's allergic reaction or a diabetic situation. I acted pretty cool when I opened the package. However, this was not an EpiPen, and the syringe appeared empty. I kinda looked at it and asked again if the doctor had said it was ready to use. Thankfully, Mrs. Beam remembered that the medicine was in another part of their bag. I was glad she remembered before I injected Mr. Beam with what appeared to me to be an invisible potion. She produced a vial that said it was B12 but looked more like straight Red Bull.

I began the process of drawing the bright-red liquid into the syringe like I knew what I was doing. After emptying the vial and thumping the syringe to get rid of the air bubbles (a trick I learned from watching *Marcus Welby, MD* as a youth), I was ready. The last shot I received, someone pinched my skin together; so, after swabbing with an alcohol pad, I did the same. A moment later, I had poked through the skin of the arm and released the medicine. It did not even bleed, although we placed a Ninja Turtles bandage featuring Rafael wielding his famous sais over it anyway.

The next few hours saw Mr. Beam endear himself to the folks on Lanai, especially the ones at the beach. He bravely made the walk to Lanai City (about a mile) for breakfast the next morning and was seemingly ready to try and avenge his lopsided defeat to Mrs. Beam at the golf game. Poor ole Mr. Beam, not even a Red Bull booster shot could enhance his putt-putt prowess enough from getting clobbered once again by the pure-precision putting of the steady-handed Mrs. Beam. It seems he had already forgotten that this lady was also the one who took care of the demon squirrels in the backyard. I believe Mr. Beam, somewhere between the course and the room, mentioned he may have "lost" the scorecard.

Author's note: The conservative Mr. Beam enjoys the beauty, scenery, and the shade of a beach umbrella when visiting the ocean. His attire, however, is totally unique. Let's see, how do you describe it but

"Beamlike." The shirt chosen for the Lanai beach was a short-sleeve dress shirt with a button-down collar. The bright-green and light-blue plaid colors, enhanced by the gorgeous deep-blue Pacific Ocean waters, were a brilliant choice to contrast against the imported white sand and black lava rock of the beaches. Under the shirt, he wore a white "wife-beater" T-shirt for that rugged manly look. He wore long black dress slacks with a black belt, black socks, and soft black leather shoes. I think he subscribes to the sports theory that you surprise the opposition with black shoes. They make you appear slower than you are. It really works for him, as he looks snaillike when Mrs. Beam, in her white sneakers, walks circles around him. He occasionally sported a red-and-white cap featuring a famous mouse and the word Mickey on the front. Normal beach attire was not in his comfort level, as he created his own style for the cabana boys and the other guests to discuss and enjoy.

Mr. Beam—Cabana Boy!

News flash from Manele Bay, Lanai—a gentleman in his mid-seventies with a strange accent and a big smile has been included into the exclusive cabana boy brotherhood at the Four Seasons Resort at Manele Bay. The members of this club are traditionally in their late teens to early twenties, with muscular builds and strong tans. The workload can be strenuous as they provide for the many guests all of their beach needs. They set up the large umbrellas, tables, and chairs. They run up the half-mile incline to the pool grill, retrieving the food the guests have ordered during the day.

It is believed Mr. Beam is the first pasty-white-skinned, only-slightly-muscled man to be invited in. "It all started when Mr. Beam came to the beach in the now Facebook-famous beach attire," said Jay, one of the leaders of the group. "I mean, not only the beach slacks but those black shoes. Not everyone can pull that off."

While the attire had something to do with it, Kai, another cabana boy, mentioned Mr. Beam's attitude. "Me and the guys were kidding each other about one of the guests"—an attention-grabbing young lady—"and did not know anyone was around to hear it. When I turned around, there was Mr. Beam, just smiling and laughing along with us. (Note: Family members traveling with Mr. Beam are pretty certain that he did not hear a word they were saying.) I mean, Mr. Beam is so cool. He had our backs."

It is also rumored that Mr. Beam was going from umbrella to umbrella shining beach shoes for the guests and telling stories, making people laugh.

Jay then said, "We think we do a lot for the people here, taking them cold rags, bringing water, pineapple, and smoothies—and then Mr. Beam shows up and makes them laugh by being himself. He had us rolling when he threatened to show up in his Speedo if we got out of line. We learned a lot from this guy in two days. We had to bring him into the group."

Author's note: The 2014 Hawaii trip followed a 2013 trip to Boston and up to Maine. The next story references the flight home.

Mr. Beam Goes Through Security

I write this post with my head resonating with questions that need to be—must be—answered. To start this deceptive tale of twists and turns, we must turn back the clock to August 2013, to a seemingly innocent moment in the airport in Bangor, Maine. I guess it is at this time that I must share something. Mr. Beam has a secret. His hair never moves. It could be a forty-miles-per-hour wind, and it stays put. And the reason is, he uses—hair spray (we will not, at this time, mention the brand, as he is awaiting endorsement deals). He not only uses hair spray, but he uses a whole lot. He uses as much spray to coat his hair as he does jelly to coat a piece of toast (and that is an overabundance). That leads to part of the dilemma. He travels with a can of hairspray so big that it needs its own suitcase, and on that fateful day in Bangor, he tried to slip it onto the plane in his carry-on luggage.

He was quickly taken aside. The bag was searched (I don't remember if dogs came and sniffed or not). It took two security officers to lift the huge canister of hair spray and hurl it into a wastebasket as they were reprimanding Mr. Beam. Mr. Beam gave them that cabana-boy smile and charm and melted the security team. They let him pass through, and everyone chuckled at the whole ordeal. As a matter of fact, his daughter (we will still call her Karen) and the favorite son-in-law had a can of hair spray waiting for Mr. Beam on his kitchen table when he got home.

Seems all innocent, doesn't it? I figured after the Bangor incident, Mr. Beam would be on some sort of government watch list, but who knew? Fast-forward to yesterday at the Lanai airport. Mrs. Beam went through security, and bells went off. She had to go back through. They checked her purse, asking if anything sharp was in the bag that they should be aware of. She said no (keep this in mind). Then it happened. Mr. Beam placed his carry-on bag on the conveyor. The security personnel eyed it suspiciously and then pulled it off to hand-check the bag. Calling Mr. Beam over, they removed a huge container of hair spray (aggghhhh, not again).

The next few details are a whirlwind. The smile, the Southern charm, it all looks to be true, but now I wonder even to myself, why is this man insistent on taking hair spray on the plane? Is he going to spray the crew in the eyes and take over the plane? Is Mr. Beam some sort of James Bond (kinda like Roger Moore in the later years)? Is he going to produce some sort of spark on the plane and make a flamethrower? Or is he really a nice man with an over-obsession for well-groomed hair, clean shoes, and sweets? And what about Mrs. Beam being taken aside? Was she in on it, trying to get one of Mr. Beam's hygiene canisters on board for him? It is all so confusing. All I know is that when we arrived at the Lihue airport on Kauai, I think I saw his photo at the security checkpoint and another by a police sketch artist of what Mr. Beam might look like without hair spray and with the trade-wind-blown look of the islands. I have also seen people around the resort in sunglasses, some hiding behind books, towels, newspapers, and even on the beach in lounge chairs, trying not to look obvious. But I know it is the CIA, FBI, Homeland Security, or maybe even the men in black checking on the man we know as Mr. Beam.

Two things I know: the Beams, upon arrival, immediately went and bought—hair spray. And second, the trip home could be an adventure. So who is this man of mystery? How has he been able to be retired for so long? Is he really retired, or a spy of some kind? Are Karen and his favorite son-in-law enablers? Only he and Mrs. Beam know for sure.

Mr. Beam and the Breakfast Buffet

As Mr. Beam neared the island of Kauai, the daughter we will still call Kathy and his second favorite son-in-law were explaining some of the differences between the islands and what to expect at the Marriott Beach Resort. One thing seemed to stand out above all the others. The beautiful foliage on the Garden Isle certainly was of interest, but the tales of the breakfast buffet brought him to an unsurpassed level of excitement. He hid his disappointment well when the plane landed on the island at 1:00 p.m. during lunch hour and after the breakfast buffet had been picked clean and put away for the day. It would be nineteen hours before it returned, and he vowed he would be ready.

Setting his clock minutes before the ceremonial cracking of the first omelet egg, he arrived to see that the staff was making the final preparations. The icing of the food was a tedious task for the staff due to the tropical climate, but they strategically managed to place the cubes in the perfect places and with awesome visual presentation touches. Finally, the buffet was complete and ready for the patrons. I do not think the hostess or staff could prepare them for what happened next. Mr. Beam gazed around the room, absorbing all the sights and smells. Wow! Look at the fruit section, an omelet station, eggs Benedict, all sorts of breakfast meats, a cereal bar with oatmeal, and so many toppings it would take hours to try them all. What were these new exotic items, such as fried rice with pork, breakfast sushi, and kimchi? His head was spinning as, for the first time on the trip, he moved fast, rushing in front of Mrs. Beam with cheetah-like speed—so fast, in fact, that his hair actually blew in the wind and was slightly misaligned. With youth-like dexterity, he got to their table, grabbing two plates and a bowl so he could get going.

And then it happened. It was like the heavens opened up, and the sun shone down on the bread, pastry, and sweet section of the bar. Mr. Beam just stood there for a moment, unable to take it all in. It reminded those who witnessed it of Ralphie in *A Christmas Story* when his eyes captured the vision of the Red Ryder BB gun, except instead of worrying about shooting your eye out, Mrs. Beam began warning Mr. Beam about the dangers of overindulging and being sick. It was too late; the words fell on deaf ears (literally).

Mr. Beam was off in a flash, piling his plate with break-neck speed and craftsmanlike precision. Not another morsel could be contained on the plate, one of many to come. As a matter of fact, the first plate was so heavy that it took both hands to carry the load, and he was short of breath when he reached the table. Fortunately, he found enough air to begin the onslaught—beginning with pancakes covered with guava jelly and mango syrup, then a two-egg omelet and slices of bacon, and continuing with pastries, topping them with syrup and jellies as well. It was machinelike. No birds even got close to Mr. Beam at this open-air restaurant overlooking the pool with the ocean in the near distance, fearing their next flapping of wings could be their last, with fork tines stopping them in midflight. The staff began to scratch their heads as they refilled the syrup, jelly, and pastry containers for the other patrons.

Mr. Beam saw the dessert tray with guava cake, coffee cheesecake, and at least three other offerings. His hand was beginning to cramp from the continuous utensil lifting, but he managed to make it into the line for the desserts. He smiled and spoke to a lady in front of him. She must have sensed his weariness from piling on food, and the next thing you know, she had cut and placed a serving of each piece of cake on his plate. He smiled and thanked her as he scurried back to the table to finish off the meal.

Mr. Beam, finally stuffed, enthusiastically paid the bill for this gorgeous meal, claiming it was worth every penny and knowing that it was a breakfast connoisseur's delight. It goes without saying that Mr. Beam was not able to eat another meal that day as the warnings of Mrs. Beam began to reverberate in his brain: "If you eat all of that, you will be sick." It is true. It could and would make you sick to eat all of that, but who has the kind of willpower to pass that up? Certainly not Mr. Beam as, day after day, the breakfast bar was ravaged. It is also true that the staff, when they saw him coming, fortified the bar with extra sweets and had warning signs for people to be on the lookout for overzealous patrons.

Mr. Beam and the Hula Instructor!

Every once in a while it happens. One of those moments just slips up on you, and it is one of the pleasant times of life, a brief passing when all is at peace, at least in your little part of the world. Such a moment was happening to me on that beautiful afternoon in Kauai. I had found a chair on the beach, actually the soft manicured grass area, under the shade of a palm tree, located right beside the brownish-golden sand that made its way to the blue Pacific. The light ocean breeze was perfectly cooling the eighty-two-degree mid-May afternoon. The sounds of island birds mingled with the soft, breaking waves. Over the speakers, in the trees surrounding the not-so-far-away poolside bar, came the familiar words of Weezer's "Island in the Sun." Not bad, I thought, as I watched Mr. Beam's daughter, whom we call Kathy, show her skills at paddleboarding. Actually, I was amazed at how skillful she was at remounting the paddleboard every few minutes as she cooled herself (purposefully, I am sure) in the water time after time.

Moments later, things changed. Oh, people were still relaxing, and I was continuing to be entertained as a local hula dancer and instructor named Nicole made her way to the beach to help the vacationers learn a little more about the famous island dance. I must describe a stereotype here, not in a bad way. Nicole was a beautiful Polynesian lady, probably in her late twenties or early thirties. The long dark hair, the beautiful, tanned skin, and the physique of, well, a hula dancer together summoned the guests to watch her dance and teach. Smiling, I thought that this should be fun watching people like myself try to learn the art. The smile transformed to a questioning, almost terrified look as I noticed, trailing in line, not far behind Nicole was, yikes, Mr. Beam! He was in his normal beach attire of black slacks, black socks, black shoes, and—what is this?—a Hawaiian shirt. Mr. and Mrs. Beam had spent the early afternoon shopping for just the right color and style, and Mr. Beam was feeling it now. You could sense something interesting was about to happen.

The soothing sound of ukulele-induced Hawaiian music set the mood as Kathy, having conquered the art of getting on the paddleboard from the deep ocean, was now coming into shore, curious also about Nicole's coaching techniques. Mrs. Beam shook her head no, while Mr. Beam kept encouraging his wife, saying, "Go on, Martha, you can do that." He was referring to the movement Nicole's grass skirt made, swaying side to side, slowly or quite fast, depending on the beat of the hand-pounded musician's drums. Several of the guests were now feeling the flow as they began to move their hips and extend their arms from side to side, simulating the motion of the waves.

Not so suddenly, Mr. Beam made his way to the line of students. The next few minutes are a bit confusing. I could not tell by watching if Mr. Beam was the best student or the worst. Obviously, no one was keeping up with Nicole, but you did have about ten folks seemingly on a similar beat and flow—and then there was Mr. Beam on a somewhat different beat and certainly his own flow. The band seemed to catch on to Mr. Beam and his "style" of Hawaiian dance. As he got with the beat, they picked up the tempo. Mr. Beam, ever the competitor, began speeding his motion and movements as the lightning-quick hands of the drummers pounded faster and faster. Nicole was keeping a torrid pace. Mr. Beam, not to be outdone, moved faster and faster, perspiration starting to form on the forehead of his still-smiling face. His hair started to move even against the forces of the massive amounts of hair spray. This lasted for about, oh, fifteen seconds, and then he was done, hands on knees and breathing like a gold-medal miler.

Kathy and Mrs. Beam helped him over to the grassy area to watch the last few minutes of the lesson. He then confessed that all he really wanted to do was to have his picture made with Nicole. I thought that the whole cabana-boy image must have gone to his head as he strolled up to her after the lesson and asked for a photo. A large, muscular islander made his way to see what was happening. I am not sure if he thought Mr. Beam was asking for private lessons or what, but it was Nicole who eased things as she introduced her husband to Mr. Beam. Graciously, she agreed to a photo.

As Kathy got ready to snap the photo, Nicole's husband hollered, "Hey, don't forget the hang-loose wave."

The common island greeting, meaning "you are happy and all is well," is made with a little wiggle of the hand with the thumb and little finger outstretched while the other three are closed. Mr. Beam fumbled for a moment, trying to get his fingers right. At one point, I mentioned to him that he might not want to leave that one finger in that position and that someone might get the wrong idea. Finally, a photo was snapped. It showed big smiles by both as Mr. Beam endeared himself to Texas fans from all over with their famous "hook 'em horns" hand sign instead of the hang-loose wave. Oh well, another day in paradise!

Author's note: As we got to Kauai, the booster shot seemed to wear off a bit (more evidence that it was really Red Bull, and he was crashing after the high). He told everyone he was fine. After witnessing his surfboard photo and the one with Nicole, the hula dancer, it is little wonder that the man we call Mr. Beam was a bit winded. His vacationing regimen left most of his fans wanting more.

Mr. Beam and the Long Flight Home

The following timeline and flight information are true. The reason for the flight issues is being debated. However, if you have been following the vacation saga closely, I am sure that you will come to a similar conclusion as this author. It all points to one thing: Mr. Beam. Hopefully, you read about the security threat that Mr. Beam had posed to the airlines with his desire to be well-groomed at all times. Had it not been for the now-famous Facebook photo of Mr. Beam discarding his hair spray before the return trip, we might indeed all still be in Hawaii. Instead, we were in the midst of a thirty-hour return adventure that started Monday, May 12, at the Lihue Airport.

We arrived at 3:00 p.m. at the Hawaiian Air terminal with tickets to Honolulu, then an overnight flight to Dallas and on to Birmingham. We anticipated being in Albertville sometime around noon on the thirteenth. As the four of us walked up to the counter, the attendant checked our IDs. Immediately, we sensed a problem. He looked at the ID and then at Mr. Beam, then made a dash to the back to get a supervisor. We were told that we were no longer on that flight. They produced a new itinerary for us and said they could not help us—basically throwing us to the curb and saying Hawaiian Air could not help us; we would need to talk to American Airlines. Thinking quickly, it dawned on me that the last hair spray incident was with Hawaiian Air. That must be it. Mr. Beam had now been flagged as a security threat. After a few pleas for help and calls to see if anything could be done, the wait for the 10:00 p.m. flight began. We would have seven hours to wait for a plane to take us to Los Angeles, Dallas, and then Birmingham, this time to arrive home at about 4:30 p.m.

Moments later, I was told that the flight we had originally booked on to arrive at noon had been canceled. Coincidence, I am beginning to think not. It sounds like the crew saw the manifest with Mr. Beam as a passenger and boycotted it, causing a logjam from Dallas to Birmingham on the thirteenth. We seemed to be okay since we were now booked on the afternoon flight. Finally, it came time to go through security. I knew the hair spray was gone, but who knew what else Mr. Beam could come up with? Suddenly, Mr. Beam throws the "I am seventy-five years old, and I do not have to take off my shoes for inspection" card. What? Come on, Mr. Beam, just take off your shoes. (He was correct about the seventy-five-year-old rule, by the way, but Mr. Beam is actually seventy-four). *Don't skirt the rules again*, I thought. Maybe they just wanted him off the island, as they allowed him to pass but watched him closely.

It was now time for the dreaded agricultural suitcase inspection. We watched as other passengers' bags were searched and items trashed that could not be taken to the mainland. Mr. Beam's was opened. One—no, two—security personnel began to search. They felt around until they finally pulled out a bottle of some sort of golden ooze. They looked at the bottle, finally opening and sampling. Mr. Beam quickly headed toward the gate as the TSA staff threw the substance away. Honey! Aggghhhh! Mr. Beam's sweet tooth almost got him busted. You can't transport honey to the mainland. As we continued to wait in Lihue, news came that the plane that was to take us to Los Angeles would be late arriving. I was sensing a real pattern, another mutiny as the crew sought hazard pay to come and carry the gentleman known as Cabana Boy! They must have won their arbitration. A plane did arrive, but now our flight to LA was two and a half hours late leaving Kauai. The dominos were really falling. We were missing the Dallas connection, which in turn missed Birmingham. We would now arrive about 10:30 p.m. and home after midnight or early the fourteenth.

It was seemingly going smoothly in LA until we boarded the plane for Dallas. The pilot announced that the first officer was at the airport but not yet on board. Was it yet another scared crew member? The plane was completely full. It is believed that an air marshal, just in case, occupied every unsold seat. Surely, the first officer had negotiated this as he boarded, and the plane left LA some thirty minutes late.

It is interesting that as soon as the plane took off and reached cruising altitude, Mr. Beam was the first out of his seat to go to the "bathroom." You could sense restlessness as several strong-looking passengers (presumed marshals) squirmed in their seats and watched as the soft-spoken man made his way to and from his seat. The plane arrived in Dallas to a collective sigh of relief four and a half hours before the Birmingham departure. Surely, there can be no more delays. Surely, the 'Bama-based flight crew recognized one of its own in Mr. Beam, and there would be no fear. But no, even the 'Bama-bound flight crew was hesitant to climb aboard. They stayed in their arriving plane until the Birmingham-bound plane had been swept clean of any grooming products or aerosol spray devices and marshals were strategically placed in their seats. This would delay even the simplest of flights another half hour, pushing our arrival home even later.

All the delays kept the original party from being able to pick us up at such a late hour. So guess who stepped in? None other than the favorite son-in-law Joey, dropped everything to come to the rescue—and that after he had spent a week of lawn mowing, car washing, and shoe shining at the Beam's home. Even after a fantastic vacation, sometimes you just can't win!

Author's note: The following epilogue was written basically for the Facebook followers who kept track of the day-to-day steps and missteps of Mr. Beam. The social media format created quite a buzz for Mr. Beam as he arrived back in Albertville and people mentioned enjoying the stories, encouraging him and Mrs. Beam to share more adventures in the future. But as is the case with life, while we were enjoying our time, friends suffered losses and had victories. I just wanted to wrap my arms around them with a cyber hug with these words.

Epilogue to Hawaii Trip for Facebook Followers

I want to thank God for allowing Kathy and me the opportunity to spend this time with Mr. and Mrs. Beam. Mr. Beam has been battling shingles and fatigue but has been a warrior (a Hawaiian Rainbow Warrior). He has shared smiles with everyone, and he and Mrs. Beam have made this special for us. You guys have also made it special. I certainly have enjoyed writing the accounts, but your witty comments and encouragement have made it that much more fun. It is like we are a big Facebook family. Mr. and Mrs. Beam had no idea what I was writing because they do not Facebook, but I have not heard them laugh as hard as they did when Kathy read them "Mr. Beam Goes through Security." The ability for us all to laugh together and for Mr. Beam to laugh at himself is priceless.

While we were away, we had friends lose loved ones and others sharing in special reunions and celebrations. Sorry we were not there, but our thoughts were and are with you all. God made a masterpiece when He created Hawaii, but He is creating a place in heaven for all of his believers that is even more amazing. I hope to see each one of you there someday. If you are not sure that you will be there, message me, and I will try to point you in heaven's direction. Thanks for sharing and being a part of our trip.

God bless!

Authors note: The next few stories are just part of everyday life. We all have those family moments. Mr. Beam just seems to put himself in a position where unusual and humorous events flow freely. Many of the stories relate to a specific event but were not written immediately. I typically wrote them as a holiday approached. For example, the Mother's Day story, of course, happened on Mother's Day but was written a few weeks later for Memorial Day weekend, and then they were shared on Facebook. This first story was another one written on Christmas Eve.

I had help from my son Alex, who was home for the holiday from his gig as an instructor for the Auburn University Rural Studio. He spends his spare time writing and recording songs. I was having trouble arranging some of the ideas. Alex and I began to bounce thoughts back and forth, laughing and carrying on. Kathy would just roll her eyes at the nonsense. There are many families out there where the men outnumber the mom. On many occasions, Kathy has had to withstand the verbal nonsense and fun at her expense from Gabe, Alex, and me. We learned early on that not only can she take a good kidding, but she can throw it right back at you. Enjoy!

Mr. Beam's Little Secret!

Most families hide little tidbits of information from the world around them. *Family secrets* are the way they are described by most. Some are a little humorous, some are weird, and some will surprise you, and that is the case here. You see, my friends, the wonderful Mr. Beam has a secret addiction that no one has yet talked about. It is not sweets; we all know about that. It has been mentioned many times in stories and folklore about how he uses jelly to flavor his syrup, which enhances the powdered sugar for his French toast. It is not even the fact that he has an unusual amount of money invested in hair spray stock; for those who know him, that goes without saying as well. This particular secret is an absolute addiction, and it is time to come clean for all you wonderful readers. Mr. Beam, plain and simple, is a— buttermilkaholic! There, I said it, and it is out. I feel better, and maybe after a year or two Mr. Beam will speak to me again. I just believe the whole family will feel better not having the pressure of keeping it hidden any longer.

It apparently started at an early age. He took his first sip at age six. I am not sure if he slipped to the icebox and turned up the milkman-delivered bottle when his parents were not looking, or if they ran out of regular milk and that was the only available semi-liquid to go with the evening meal. All we can surmise is that once he tasted the putrid substance, he was hooked. Over the next seven decades, Mr. Beam not only has developed an aversion to regular milk but has become an expert on all things buttermilk. According to Mr. Beam, a great glass of buttermilk, when poured, will have five "clumps" fall into the glass for an eight-ounce serving. He also has his favorite brands and has learned what time of year each company comes up with its best-tasting conglomeration.

For example, according to the connoisseur, Barber's buttermilk is best in April and May before the bitterweed takes hold in the pastures of the milk cows. Meadow Gold, he says, is perfect for fall due to the golden foliage on the trees (his logic, not mine). Purity, of course, is his winter favorite, reminding him of pure white snow. Mr. Beam mentioned that Mayfield was his summer favorite. It apparently sits lighter on the stomach after the sweltering temperatures. When I mentioned that it seemed, based on his Meadow Gold and Purity logic, that Mayfield should be his spring favorite because of the name, he just stared at me like I did not know the first thing about buttermilk and I should keep my opinions about the subject to myself.

I must stop for a moment and confess that he is right. I know nothing, nor do I wish to know anything, about buttermilk. I just like good cooks to use it for making biscuits and pancakes, but I feel under no circumstances should you drink the stuff. Mr. Beam denies that he is actually addicted to the buttermilk. He says that he uses it for "medicinal purposes" and that it "soothes his stomach." But his body's reaction and his actions may indicate something more complex. A lot of addictions have withdrawal symptoms, so apparently does buttermilk. Our 2013 trip to Maine brought this to full light.

It had been three days since our flight took us from the comfort of our Alabama homes to Boston. We had made the drive up to Portsmouth, New Hampshire, for a conference that I was attending. Mr. and Mrs. Beam had been all smiles and having a great time as they strolled with the daughter we will call Kathy and me around the picturesque seaside town. After a short stay, we drove up the coast to Bar Harbor, Maine. On our first evening in the tourist-friendly locale, Mr. Beam began to drag a little, showing signs of fatigue. Mrs. Beam whispered to Kathy, "Jerry is in need of some buttermilk." It had been three days since he had any, and he was starting to feel it.

As we strolled back to the bed and breakfast after our evening meal and ice cream, we stopped in several small shops, convenience stores, etc. I made Mr. Beam ask for the stuff. Mr. Beam, with the soft-spoken Southern accent, got quite a few raised eyebrows when he asked the clerk if they had any buttermilk in the back. "Buttermilk!" they would exclaim. "We don't sell stuff like that here!" We were striking out everywhere, and Mr. Beam was beginning to get slower and slower. It was buttermilk, and only buttermilk, that could get this man going again. He needed a buttermilk fix badly.

Finally, I asked one interesting-looking guy on the street corner if he knew where I could get some buttermilk. He said, "Man, what are you talking about? I know where you can get some beanies, hash, or blow, but I have never heard of buttermilk."

I quickly said, "Thanks for the help," and scooted on my way.

Kathy heard someone mention a supermarket about a block away, and we took our chances. Finally, Mr. Beam located, in the back dimly lit corner of the cooler, a small carton. It was a Bulgarian buttermilk known as Darigold, supposedly a gourmet buttermilk. We had the clerk place it in a brown paper bag so we could complete our stroll without anyone knowing what we had purchased. It was a little sad to see Mr. Beam every thirty steps or so turning up the brown bag, taking a drink and then wiping his mouth with his sleeve. After finishing half the container, he was sound asleep. The next morning, I will say that he did seem to feel great as he put away his supersized breakfast.

You would have thought that the four of us would have learned something from the Maine experience, but alas, in May of 2014, Mr. Beam once again found himself in a buttermilk withdrawal, this time on the island of Kauai in Hawaii. Again at night, and again the quest for the desired fix. This time, we were a bit more aggressive in finding the buttermilk. It was in a store right next to the "spirits" section—hmmm!

Author's note: I wrote the buttermilk story on Christmas Eve for friends to enjoy. I finished with the following lines: Merry Christmas to everyone, and tonight, instead of that Christmas Eve eggnog toast, let's face Howard Avenue and toast Mr. Beam with a cold glass of buttermilk. Actually, let's not do that. (I know I will not, yeck!)

Mr. Beam and the Visitation!

The South—for those of us who live here and love it here, we know just how much the customs and traditions mean to a people group that understands that when you mention *Bear* and *Shug*, you are talking about men.

A sad part for the ones who remain here on this earth is the passing of a loved one. Those of us who have been through the tough times of losing someone have been a part of standing as friends and acquaintances form a long line to greet and comfort you in your time of loss—*the visitation*. When we hear of a loss, we find out the arrangements and usually make a decision to go to the visitation, the actual funeral, or both. Mr. and Mrs. Beam have always been kind, compassionate, caring, and they make sure they get by to console their friends in times of sorrow.

Not long ago, after hearing yet another name that struck the chords of their heartstrings leaving this world, they planned their trip to the funeral home for the visitation. Now, with the Beams, this is a production. Had they lived in Bible times, they could have probably passed for those professional mourners the preachers tell us about, but they do it out of kindness. Mr. Beam is going to wear a suit— gotta look sharp. Not only that, but his shirt and tie are going to match whatever dress Mrs. Beam decides to wear. I take a moment here and say this is another area where I lose points. Apparently, the favorite son-in-law and the daughter, whom we will call Karen, also match their clothes on Sundays as they make their way to church. I am not sure the daughter we will call Kathy and yours truly, the second favorite, have even thought about wearing matching outfits.

The Beams, looking sharp, got into their Lincoln with the tag on the front that says, "Sweet Momma," (Don't ask. I never have, and am not sure I want to know) and prepared to comfort the family. They walked into the moderately crowded funeral home (they had come early to beat the long lines). They saw and greeted other church members and friends in line. They shared stories and prayer requests. Finally, they got to the point where they went over to the casket and looked at the deceased. (I never have understood the "don't they look natural?" comments. I guess because, to me, they don't.) They then turned to the family, offered their condolences, and assured them they would continue to pray for them.

As they got back in the car and started to leave, Mr. Beam broke the silence, saying, "That really surprised me."

Mrs. Beam quizzed him, "What do you mean?"

He just looked at her and said, "I didn't know him or any of them; never seen them before."

Mrs. Beam said, "Well, I was wondering, because I did not know them either. I thought you did."

Sometimes I just shake my head.

Mr. Beam and the Seventy-Fifth-Birthday Lunch

The ever-thoughtful Mr. Beam had parked his early 90s Dodge Ram pickup on his front lawn so that others could use the driveway and have easy entry and exit to the home hosting the noonday seventy-fifth-birthday feast prepared by Mrs. Beam for her spouse. The pickup, the color of a ripe Maine blueberry, shone like a beacon to the arriving family members as it sat on the beautiful green grass that once again measured precisely one and a half inches high.

I tried to get there a little early but could not beat the favorite son-in-law, his wife, whom we will call Karen, Zac, Cassie Jo, and yes, Kinlie Jo (the three-month-old who erased all the brownie points that I had made with Mr. Beam in Hawaii). The daughter we will call Kathy, Gabe, and Hannah, all made it as well.

Mrs. Beam requested the favorite son-in-law to ask a blessing. Boy, did he take advantage of that. Not only does he pastor a church, but as he prayed, he did not miss a thing. He thanked God for Mr. Beam's wonderful seventy-five years, his dedication to his family, his faithfulness in leading his family in a Godly manner, and even for improved health. I could not help but think that Mr. Beam was adding all those points to the favorite's side, so I did all I could. I said "amen" real fast and loud when the prayer was over, letting Mr. Beam know I agreed with all that.

There was plenty to eat: wonderful roast and vegetables, salads, and of course Mr. Beam's favorite—the desserts. Mrs. Beam had made a yellow cake with caramel icing, angel food cake, and cut-up strawberries (yum). Kathy had brought some peanut brittle that she had purchased from the Church of God ladies. I don't know what it is with denominations and special skills, but the Methodists (at least Hewett Memorial) make fantastic cornbread, soup, and salads. The Baptists are known for frying chicken, the Catholics work wonders with seafood and gumbo, and both the Presbyterians and Episcopalians sure know how to smoke Boston butts. However, when it comes to peanut brittle (and banana bread), you can't beat the Church of God.

Mr. Beam started the dessert architectural wonder. A large round piece of peanut brittle covered the bottom of the plate. On top of that was a piece of caramel cake on one half and angel food cake on the other. Strawberries covered the structure like a red metal roof on a two-story house. Before he dug in, he opened his gifts. His eyes got big when he peeled back the paper revealing a jar filled with amber-colored liquid with a waxy-looking piece in the middle.

"Oh boy, honey," he exclaimed, and he started unscrewing the lid to add the perfect topping to his creation.

At the last minute, Karen stopped him, explaining that it was not honey. It was Island of the Sea sea salt scrub, cucumber melon. I believe Mr. Beam only heard "cucumber melon" as he once again moved it toward his plate.

"No!" Karen exclaimed. "It is for your hands to help calluses and to keep them smooth."

He paused and lowered the jar. He did not say it, but suddenly I smiled, knowing that we had brought the wonderful peanut brittle, and the favorite had brought nonedible hand sanitizer. The scoreboard was tilting back—yes!

Mr. Beam and the Yard Sale

Black Friday means different things to different folks. If you talk to the Wall Street people, they mention the ugly stock market turns of Octobers past. For retailers, it is the glorious day after Thanksgiving when the nation goes crazy at the start of the Christmas shopping season. If you happen to live around Albertville and you are tuned in to the wild world of yard sales, Black Friday means one thing— Mr. Beam is having one of his two annual yard sales, and you better be there early. Yes, so popular is this event that it happens twice a year, once in the spring and again in the fall.

Mr. Beam prepares for the events like a squirrel storing nuts for the winter. Week after week, he is up before daylight and quick to respond to all the area yard sales, estate sales, rummage sales, bingo events—you name it (maybe bingo is a stretch). After weeks of gathering, he looks for a date to market his goods. He does not trust the long-range forecast on smartphones, so he consults the *Farmer's Almanac* to make sure the weekend will be perfect. It is also widely rumored that he asks his favorite son-in-law to pray for the weather as well, seeing if Pastor Joey still has all the good pull with the Man Upstairs.

Mr. Beam's warehouse (storage building) in the backyard is busting with merchandise. He gets the proper permits from the city. He does not understand why they are always "picking on him and concerned about his signage." After investigating this, it was determined that the city has to have an extra policeman on duty to handle Terrace Heights traffic control during the event, thus the concern. When the announcement goes public, the whole neighborhood takes off work, realizing they can make more money using their yards for five dollars per car parking spots and shuttle service to the yard sale than they can at work.

The day of the event arrived, and I decided to go by and check things out for myself. Of course, the October Friday was a gorgeous day. I circled the block a few times and then saw a gentleman with a clipboard and a camera getting into an old beat-up pickup truck with an Arkansas tag reading WALTON 5. It appears a national retailer had been by to get ideas about the way things should operate. I waited for him to exit and raced into the parking space, barely beating a 1977 Chevy van with shag carpet on the walls and ceiling.

As I walked up, I noticed the grass appeared once again to be the perfect one and a half inches tall. Mrs. Beam (the ever-friendly greeter and hostess) was welcoming everyone. She offered shopping boxes to anyone who would like one and pointed people into the different sections of the driveway and yard. Mr. Beam had used the cabana-boy charm to talk two neighbors into helping with the event. We will call them Shawna and Dewanna. He promised them all the collection of Coke merchandise and who knows what else for their efforts. They patrolled the aisles, aiding the shoppers with their selection. Mr. Beam was on an elevated deck, observing—the eye in the sky, some may say; a lifeguard protecting the beach, others might think. He stood there smiling, answering questions, and wearing the Mickey Mouse baseball cap with more buttons on it than a lucky fisherman's hat has lures. My personal favorite button says, "Aloha."

The aisles were spacious, and the tables were well-decorated. Clothes were in one section, games in another; kitchen accessories, hardware, art supplies, and entertainment all had their own spots. There was even a Christmas section. The time and effort of unwrapping the seven layers of newspaper and plastic from each piece of glassware was worth the effort. It looked fantastic! No prices were marked. "Offer what you want to" pricing, Mr. Beam calls it. Shoppers were ecstatic at the bargains, and although all the signs were in one language, no one had trouble with communication at the Mr. Beam yard sale. Jolly ole Mr. Beam, like his Christmas counterpart, can communicate in all languages.

When the weekend was over, the tables were empty, and the customers were satisfied, Mr. Beam looked at Mrs. Beam and said, "Thanks once again for your help, sweet momma. We get to do it again in the spring."

I am sure that your Black Friday experience will be every bit as enjoyable. Happy Thanksgiving!

Author's note: It is said that pride comes before the fall. I am guilty as charged. As my fifty-six years have taken a toll on my physical appearance and my once-brown hair is almost white, I have been pleased that my passion for tennis has kept me physically able to run and play sports with warriors half my age. You could say that I was proud. In February of 2015, I was humbled, as I had a complete tear of my Achilles tendon while playing basketball. The injury would require surgery and take me out of action for six months. Some of the stories reference my limited abilities.

The following story did take place on Mother's Day in early May, but I wrote and posted it on Memorial Day.

Mr. Beam and the Mother's Day Drone!

Wow! Mother's Day 2015—a beautiful sunny day in the heart of Sand Mountain. The satellites orbiting high above the earth could not have picked a more pleasant spot to zoom their super telephoto lens than the backyard of Mr. Beam's favorite son-in-law and his wife, whom we will call Karen. I gotta hand it to him. I had no chance. Everything was perfect! The burgers and hot dogs from the grill were fantastic. Brother-in-law Joey had even enlisted the help of the ladies with the excellent side dishes. The lawn looked like a golf course, bringing a smile to Mr. Beam. Even the water temperature of the crystal-clear pool registered a very comfortable upper eighties, which was perfect for the swimmers among us. Gabe swam a bit, as did Cassie. Joey was even in the water with Kinlie Jo when Kathy and I arrived. Mr. and Mrs. Beam, along with Mr. and Mrs. Cannady, Hannah, Zac, and later, Kadin, watched from swings and chairs in the shade. If Norman Rockwell was still looking for Americana to showcase his strokes of genius, this Mother's Day scene would be such a place.

Joey's strategy was so well planned that he appointed me to ask God's blessing on the meal. I did my best but realized that by asking me to pray on Mother's Day, Joey knew he would get Father's Day and lay it on about Mr. Beam. Boy, is he devious. I have to admit it was all good. The meal was great, with homemade ice cream. Shoot, he and Zac had even planned a little entertainment. Zac had recently received a drone as a gift. Now, because of *Star Wars*, I thought a drone was like R2-D2 or C-3PO. I have not warmed to the idea of little, tiny aircraft hovering low to the ground or flying high, taking pictures of whatever may be seen. It seems Joey enjoyed Zac's drone so much that he purchased one of his own. These are not the airplane-shaped drones with wings. They are about the size and shape of a canned ceiling light with four tiny propellers that help it change direction quickly. The person flying the drone uses a remote control, and the drone goes and goes until the battery dies. The lights on the drone begin to blink, giving you a little warning that it needs to be recharged. During this time, it becomes a little harder to control.

Joey and Zac asked everyone to come to the side yard for the exhibition. Using the remote, Joey looked like he did back in the day playing *Donkey Kong* at the local arcade. He was in control. That drone was in his power. Shoot, one time, he had it hovering right at my nose. It sounded like a bunch of bees. I was thinking of running, but the lack of a strong left Achilles tendon left me powerless. I had to stand there, not sure what humiliation this drone was about to cause me. Then I noticed the lights starting to flash. I did have a close-up view. About that time, Zac encouraged Joey to show us all how high it could go. In a jiff, the drone left my sight line, and all our necks were strained as we stared up as high as we could with our hands covering our eyes to shield the bright evening sun. Joey did a few loop-the-loops and then brought it rapidly back toward the crowd.

Suddenly, the drone shot a direct line for the group. I figured Joey was about to make it stop and hover, giving Mr. Beam a little thrill, but at the last moment, I sensed something was amiss. The drone accelerated into the crowd and crashed into Mr. Beam, striking him just below the elbow. Mr. Beam stunned, Joey speechless, Zac laughing, and me thinking, *Boy, did Joey blow those brownie points*—all happened in a millisecond. Then I saw the blood gushing (trickling) from the gaping wound (scratch), and I quickly sprinted (hobbled) to see if I could help, maybe get a tourniquet (Band-Aid) to help Mr. Beam recover. He reassured everyone, much to Zac's disappointment, that we did not need to call MedFlight (Zac enjoys watching the rescue team). He bravely stood there as Joey searched for a missing propeller (which was probably buried deep in Mr. Beam's arm) like he would search for his missing sermon notes before a big revival meeting.

As it turns out, no stitches were required, and the drone still flies. We learned two new things from the experience: First, beware of the Cannady drones if you live in Terrace Heights, and second, the best time to leave the field of play is when the scoreboard is in your favor!

Have a great Memorial Day and *thank you* to all who have sacrificed and served for our freedom!

Mr. Beam and the Father's Day Gone Bad

Author's Note: This story was written about our Father's Day in June but placed on Facebook on the Fourth of July.

The two weeks leading up to Father's Day featured Kathy and me moving from our Northridge home of twenty-two years to a home closer to Mr. and Mrs. Beam in Terrace Heights. After the Mother's Day droning and the move closer to Mr. Beam, I felt I was well on my way to taking over the number-one son-in-law spot. It should have been a clue to me when Mr. Beam would tell folks that, since I had moved closer to him, he was moving to Guntersville (a neighboring city to our Albertville hometown). Shoot, I thought he was joking, but after Father's Day, I am not so sure.

Kathy and I hustled to get things in place so that we could host the gathering. We don't have a pool like the other guy, so I knew we were playing from behind. After the not-so-healthy but delicious burgers and dogs on Mother's Day, we decided to show how we wanted Mr. Beam to stick around for many more Father's Days by serving—well, salad. Now, granted, these were very hearty salads. There was also a separate egg salad. We had a little lean turkey, grits, and shrimp as well. Mr. Beam must have caught wind of the menu, because he chose to bring not one but two freezers of homemade ice cream, peach and Oreo. I am not sure he could stand the thought of eating a meal with no sweets to complement the cuisine. I gotta admit, I was not complaining; the ice cream was quite tasty. But so much for the longevity meal—it is always "eat sweets like there is no tomorrow" for Mr. Beam.

Kinlie Jo was garnering most of the after-dinner attention. Cassie, Kadin, Joey, the daughter we will call Karen, Gabe, Hannah, Mr. and Mrs. Beam, the daughter we will call Kathy, and I watched as Zac rode Kinlie around in his wheelchair from room to room. I was lost in thought, thinking about what would happen next and anxiously awaiting Mr. Beam opening the Father's Day gifts.

We had borrowed the bright-blue pickup from Mr. Beam for many of the crosstown box-relocating trips. I had noticed the "Sweet Momma" tag on Mrs. Beam's car and also recognized that the truck had nothing to identify its main driver. Then I devised a plan, a surefire way to move me up that needed notch in likeability. I decided I would give him two gifts: one from me, and the other, I would say, from Joey. With help from my coworker (and, in this case, my cohort in crime) Emily Jennings, we designed car tags for the front of the truck that would identify Mr. Beam to all who would meet him on the roads. One such tag would have a note designating Joey as the giver. The note would say things like, "I saw this and thought of you, and you are awesome," things that Joey would say. The tag itself was white with the head of a junkyard dog and black letters spelling the bold words "Mean Daddy," the perfect complement to the "Sweet Momma" tag. I smiled to myself as I imagined the raised eyebrows when Mr. Beam looked at Joey, questioning the gift. For the tag from me, Emily designed a fun-loving, good-looking guy in a Hawaiian shirt laughing, with the words "The Amazing Mr. Beam" in the perfect blue to match the truck. Of course, my card also said something like, "I saw this and thought of you."

Now came opening time. There were a couple of other gifts around. I decided to hold back the tags. Mr. Beam opened a nice gift from the daughter we will call Kathy, and then Zac handed him one. He opened the gift, held it up, and my jaw surely hit the floor. Mr. Beam was now the proud, almost giddy owner of a taser—yes, a handheld. knock-you-for-a-loop taser! I could not grasp what had happened, and for the next five minutes, Mr. Beam threatened to tase Hannah. Why? No one knows. Then Zac grabbed it, had it set to stun, and was swinging wildly at anybody within reach, especially his mom. I have yet to understand the gift. It can't be for protection. No offense to Mr. Beam, but he is not fast enough to chase down anyone, and his bones creak too loudly for him to sneak up on someone to zap them. The only thing I could think of was a squirrel. Since he could not hit one shooting at it with an air rifle, maybe he could tase one.

My head was still shaking at all the things that could go wrong with that last gift, but he seemed happy. Then he opened the next gift from the Cannady contingent. When I saw it, only three words crossed my mind, *What the heck*? It was mace! Mace . . . mace . . . I could not make things compute. Why would you give this guy mace? He will only point it in the wrong direction or spray it into the wind. This was just not good. Was he going to first mace the squirrels so that they would be disoriented and then tase them? What was wrong with everybody? Kinlie Jo probably couldn't wait to play with the black desert scorpions that her granddaddy and uncle were sure to get her for Christmas this year. I felt like I had become a part of the Addams family. After these gifts, I expected Joey (Gomez) to blow up a toy train or Uncle Zac (Fester) to put a lightbulb in his mouth.

I finally steadied myself and decided it was now time to open the tags. The first tag was the "Mean Daddy" tag from "Joey." Boy, did I blow it! Mr. Beam loved it. He acted as if he liked the second "Amazing" tag as well, but I was not convinced.

Things began to calm down inside the home until Zac saw a bunny rabbit hopping innocently along in the neighbor's yard. Before I knew it, he had convinced Mr. Beam to load up the weapons and try to practice on the garden-eating herbivore. They chased it from yard to yard. After, oh, about two and a half minutes, Mr. Beam started wheezing, and I thought for just a moment that he was going to use the mace as an inhaler. Thankfully, Mrs. Beam stopped him. Moments later, I got a slight reprieve. As they turned to walk toward home, Zac ran over Mr. Beam's foot with his wheelchair (all 360 pounds, plus Zac, of it). Seeing the pain and agony, I rushed to offer my recently discarded crutches to the wounded father of my wife, eager to help in any way I could.

The lesson this day is simple: never give your adversary something that can be used in battle; it can come back to bite you. What I thought would be a no-brainer choice of "The Amazing Mr. Beam" tag was very much in question. Do I really just not know the man? Did I really just push Joey even further out front? How can it be? Mr. Beam does not seem to see the truth—Joey flies a drone into him, Zac runs over his foot, and then they give him weapons of minimal destruction. They obviously do not want the Beams to go on any more trips with me. How can Mr. Beam possibly go through security with a taser, mace, and a supersized can of hair spray? Joey and Zac—those two are devious, I tell you, doing anything to keep the number one ranking. Any suggestions to help me would be appreciated.

Have a great Fourth, everyone! God bless the USA!

Mr. Beam Goes to Washington!

Author's note: The annual convention that had us in Maine in 2013 decided to meet in Annapolis, Maryland, in 2015. Sensing an opportunity, Kathy and I asked Mr. and Mrs. Beam to join us for a week in Maryland. We would start in Annapolis and drive over to Washington, DC, to see the nation's capital. We also decided to drive on this trip. I could not come to a conclusion that would make going through the rigors of security with the well-groomed, well-armed Mr. Beam worth the risk. Actually, I had just purchased a new car that I wanted to drive. The next few stories deal with our Maryland adventures.

Mr. Beam's Walk Around Washington (Monument)

"Look!" I exclaimed as we approached our hotel in downtown Washington on Pennsylvania Avenue, a mere block and a half from the White House. "They are welcoming you back, Mr. Beam."

I was joking, of course, but probably somewhere in the back of his mind, Mr. Beam thought for just a moment that the sign being waved by a citizen along the roadside read, "Welcome back, Mr. Beam." After all, it had only been fifty-eight years since his last trip to the nation's capital, and he remembered everything so well, especially the flowering cherry trees that lined many of the streets and landmarks around the National Mall. However, as we got a little closer, the wind straightened the complete sign and showed the true words: "Welcome back, Binyamin Netanyahu," referring to Israel's prime minister. We laughed and joked for a few minutes, wondering how the citizens could overlook such a moment as the arrival of the amazing Mr. Beam.

The JW Marriott turned out to be the perfect location for what we wanted to do while in town. We wanted to play the tourists and visit the sites. The hotel is on the fourteenth block of Pennsylvania Avenue, and we all know who lives at the 1600 address of the same street. Thus, the Washington Monument, Smithsonian, and many other features were all within walking distance. Some of the walks and the hot August temperatures would stretch the endurance of the Beams, but they seemed up for the challenge, and we had enough days set aside that we could go at a controlled pace. At least that was the plan. Boy, was I wrong, as the end of day two brought a race against time and elements.

We started the day with a hearty breakfast at the buffet. The piles of French toast, pancakes, containers of syrups, jellies, and the mounds of bacon were inviting—and that was all on Mr. Beam's plate and side of the table. We then decided to take a stroll toward the Smithsonian. After visiting both the Museum of Natural History and the Museum of American History (the flag from Fort McHenry is a sight to see), we decided to split up for the afternoon. Mr. and Mrs. Beam were going to grab some lunch and head back to rest for a bit. The daughter we will call Kathy and the second favorite son-in-law were trudging onward toward the National Museum of Art, but in the back of my mind, I was concerned about the in-laws making their way back without us. I had pointed them in the proper direction and turned them loose. Kathy and I spent the next four and a half hours seeing sight after sight. We even made it across the National Mall to the Jefferson Memorial, and when we got back to the hotel at about 4:45 p.m., we were pretty tired. As a matter of fact, Kathy's phone had her with around twenty-eight thousand steps for the day. We had been back about ten minutes when the phone rang, and Mrs. Beam mentioned that they were thinking of trying to make it to the Jefferson Memorial. Kathy was done and mentioned she did not want to get back out. I volunteered to make the trip with them. I picked them up at their room, and off we went.

We exited the Marriott and headed east to start the 1.5-mile stroll to see the statue of one of my favorite presidents. We could have headed straight down Fifteenth Street, but the sidewalk scenery is just not the same as heading around the monuments. The short stroll around Pershing Park placed us behind the south lawn of the White House and right across from the site of the National Christmas Tree that stands on the north side of the playground/park known as the Ellipse. We walked the east side of the Ellipse, enjoying some of the coed softball action going on in the various sections of the park. I noticed when we passed other groups how many people spoke in a foreign language. It was astounding and a little thought-provoking. We have so many people who want to see what makes our country special, but we also have so many people out to destroy what we have. What a task to try and be the leaders of the free world, loved by many and hated by others.

At the south side of the Ellipse, we crossed Constitution Avenue and headed toward the Washington Monument. The Beams were doing well on this slight uphill portion. Mrs. Beam could really walk at a good pace; Mr. Beam was not so swift but consistent. He kind of had to lean forward to keep moving. I don't know if it was due to his unmoving hair creating a drag of major proportions or what, but staying low seemed to help him. We stayed on the eastern path of the Washington Monument and looked toward the World War II Memorial, Lincoln Memorial, the Reflecting Pool, the Vietnam Memorial, and Constitution Gardens, all of which we had visited the day before. We could now see the Jefferson Memorial and were amazed at how low the airplanes seemed as they approached their landing destination at nearby Ronald Reagan Washington National Airport. It could almost be said that the nineteen-foot-tall statue of the third president is greeting the low-flying passengers as he gazes out toward the sky and the city from the memorial.

We then made our way across the confusing Independence Avenue toward the Tidal Basin, a beautiful lake formed from the Potomac River. Mr. Beam then saw what he had hoped, and the memories came rushing forth. The cherry trees—yes, this was the area he remembered. Sure, it had changed, but his mind was going back to 1957 and the senior class trip to the district. I don't know for sure, but he must have looked over every tree as he passed them by. Maybe he had carved his initials in one or placed chewing gum on one of the branches. He never told us the intrigue about them, but it could have been no more than a moment that stirred fun times of years long ago.

Arriving at the memorial, Mrs. Beam and I dashed up the marble steps to see inside. Mr. Beam joined us several moments later. He was getting a bit tired, but he did make it up. From the top steps, we could look back toward the National Mall and the city in general. It was a great view and a few fun minutes. We were all getting recharged for the return trip.

Suddenly, in the distance, a dark cloud was in view, and bright flashes of lightning began to illuminate the sky. I found it ironic that the darkness from my view had formed over the Watergate Hotel. It certainly is not the first time a dark cloud from the Watergate challenged the DC area. The fast-moving storm appeared to be heading toward us. I casually mentioned that we might get a little wet on the return trip. I might as well have said, "On your mark, get set, go," for Mrs. Beam started down the steps like she was shot out of a cannon. I thought she said something to Mr. Beam like, "Come on, Jerry, let's go!" as she breezed by me.

Mr. Beam, stunned by the sudden burst of the fleet-footed Mrs. Beam, began to descend the stairs with tortoise-like speed. Mrs. Beam, by now, was on the path and heading toward the hotel. I did not know what to do. Do I even attempt to keep up with the pace of Mrs. Beam? Or do I ask WWJD (what would Joey do)? Heck, I knew what Joey would do. He would stay with Mr. Beam to stay the number one son-in-law and to keep from being embarrassed when he could not catch Mrs. Beam. I decided to try and stay somewhere in the middle, within eye and earshot of both of them.

As Mrs. Beam circled the Tidal Basin, it hit me why she was in such a hurry. It was her hair. She has her hair done by a wonderful beautician every Friday, and it stays "fixed" until the next session. It is a no-maintenance hairdo. The only maintenance is to not let it get wet. This was Thursday, and we were not getting back home until late weekend, creating an already heavy stress load on the normal one-week period. We had no umbrella, and she had no rain bonnet. The only way to save the style was to beat the rain, and she seemed determined to do just that.

The wind was starting to blow in the way that we had all felt before the drops hit the earth. The darkness was beginning to engulf us as the cloud moved toward the National Mall. People everywhere were scurrying, picking up lawn chairs and making their way inside. I jogged a few steps to help Mrs. Beam cross Independence Avenue, and I waited for Mr. Beam to do the same. Mrs. Beam was moving on. *Goodness,* I thought, *this is an interesting situation.* As Mr. Beam got to me, I began to be inundated with the sounds of traffic and music in passing cars. One familiar tune got closer and closer, and it was not from a passing car but from the sometime song leader from Mount Olive Baptist Church. This was no church hymn but a very familiar song from the era of his first Washington trip. This was not Chuck Berry singing "Johnny B. Goode" but Paul Jerry using the same tune but with new words. It sounded something like this:

Way down in Alabama close to Geraldine,
Way back up in the woods among the evergreens
There was a pretty girl the name of Martha Faye,
And when she smiled at me, man it made my day.
I have been with this great lady for quite a while
But I never could have guessed how fast she walked a mile.
Go, go
Go, Martha, go, go
Go, Martha, go, go
Go, Martha, go, go
Go, Martha, go, go
Martha be good!

Make sure you look both ways before you cross the street
And be careful how you smile at all the folks you meet.

All those guys from Congress sitting in the shade,
Could only come up with, "Tie your hair in a braid."
The people passing by, they would look around,
As Martha passed right by them at the speed of sound!
Go, go
Go, Martha, go, go
Go, Martha, go, go
Go, Martha, go, go
Go, Martha, go, go
Martha be good!

You know you gotta hurry, see the lightning flash,
From Thomas to the Marriott you must surely dash.
Many people scurry at the thunder's sound.
You must make the hotel lobby before the rain comes down.
Maybe tomorrow morning your hair will look just right,
It all depends on how fast you move your feet tonight.
Go, go
Go, Martha, go, go
Go, Martha, go, go
Go, Martha, go, go
Go, Martha, go, go
Martha be good!

I was shaking my head when he reached my side and mentioned that he could make some great singer a fantastic lyricist. After encouraging a little more speed from him, Mr. Beam said, "Go with Martha. I will be fine."

I told him that I would not leave him behind but would keep within shouting distance of both. As he stepped back onto the National Mall, I caught a glimpse of Mrs. Beam almost directly in front of the Washington Monument some two hundred yards ahead.

Debris was starting to blow across the park as I ran to cut down the distance between Mrs. Beam and me.

I shouted, "Mrs. Beam, I think we are losing him."

She just turned for a moment, motioned with her arm, and yelled out, "Come on, Jerry! Hurry!"

Man, I thought, *I hope we make it.* I have never seen Mrs. Beam with a decimated hairstyle, but it must be awful. If she was working this hard to avoid it, I am sure I do not want to see it.

This time, we crossed Constitution Avenue very close to Fifteenth Street, and we decided to go up the straighter path of the sidewalk rather than circling the Ellipse. One problem: this was a complete uphill grade. The lightning getting closer, the clouds moving in, the breeze getting stronger, and Mrs. Beam going faster placed quite a distance between Kathy's two parents. Mr. Beam was singing loudly from behind, "Go, go, go, Martha, go, go!" while laughing at the whole situation. I was telling Mrs. Beam that her husband was getting farther behind and asking her to slow down. Mrs. Beam, now one block from the hotel, had one thing on her mind, and that was finishing the sprint before the bottom fell out. I raced to her and helped her across the ever-busy Fifteenth Street and pointed to the lobby door of the Marriott. I then went back and waited for Mr. Beam. The man was a bit winded after the incline but had a burst of energy when the crosswalk sign flashed fifteen seconds until the light changed, leaving us as roadkill for the taxi drivers.

Finally, inside the lobby, we quickly consumed about four or five cups of the fruit water offered near the concierge stand. We had made it. The rain started a little bit later. Everyone seemed happy and tired. I believe Mrs. Beam kept a rain bonnet with her for the rest of the trip, just in case.

Mr. Beam and the Hungry Lions

William Shakespeare once wrote, "That's a valiant flea that dares eat his breakfast on the lip of a lion." And thus this story begins.

The day after our arrival, the JW Marriott became filled with guests. These were not just any guests. These were large guests. The elevators that could normally hold ten comfortably could now barely hold six. It was August in DC, and the Detroit Lions had entered the building for a preseason game against the Washington Redskins (this was before the nickname was changed to the Commanders). Now that I am middle-aged, it is a little weird to see how baby-faced all these football warriors appear in person. Don't get me wrong, they are large and intimidating, but they look young. I am a Georgia Bulldogs fan and pull for the Lions due to the former dawg Matthew Stafford being the quarterback. I am also intrigued at how well he and the archrival Georgia Tech Yellow Jacket wide receiver Calvin Johnson work together as a team. Mr. Beam does not really watch much football. The Lions could have been a group of oversized, extremely muscular dentists at a convention, as far as he could tell. He noticed my excitement about the players, but he did not know whom to look for, so we just sat for a little while in the lobby, wondering who might stroll by next. After a half hour or so, we went to our rooms, tired from a day of sightseeing.

As I have mentioned several times in the preceding chapters, it is hard to beat a Marriott breakfast buffet. They just do it right. You should find something you like, and you should not leave hungry. Mr. Beam destroys the breads and sweets on the buffet, but he also has an enormous appetite for bacon. The previous day, Mrs. Beam had tried to count the number of pieces that he consumed. On his second trip, Mrs. Beam said, "Jerry, that is seven more pieces." I never heard nor asked the total.

This morning, as he rounded the corner to the meat section of the buffet and opened the lid to the bacon, he noticed that there were not many pieces left. *Many*, in this case, is a relative term. I might consider ten to be "many," whereas to Mr. Beam, thirty might be the magical number. Concerned, he looked to his right, found a plate, and continued to pile on the bacon until the container was empty. He then took it to our table and placed it in the middle.

A few large gentlemen with shirts that read "Property of the Detroit Lions" asked the cook for some more bacon. She told them that they were beginning to prepare some more, but it would be fifteen to twenty minutes. They told her that they did not have that long, but you could see the disappointment. As they headed back to their table, they passed by our booth. One of the gentlemen with a baconless plate stopped, looked down at the pile of bacon on our table, and asked, "How's the bacon?" I wanted to hide.

Mr. Beam, thinking it was a manager, looked up, smiled, and said in his Southern accent, "It is real good, crispy and just the way I like it. I emptied the server. There was not much left, and I figured the cooks needed it emptied so they could bring more. I was more than glad to help out." I wanted to offer him a few pieces, but I knew if I did, it would only drop me further behind the favorite son-in-law in the race for Mr. Beam's approval.

A few spoonfuls of jelly on a biscuit and a couple of swigs of coffee later, Mr. Beam was ready for more strolls around town. I noticed as we got up from the table that the bacon plate was not quite empty. The quick-thinking Mr. Beam found a napkin, wrapped the remaining pieces, and placed them in Mrs. Beam's purse, claiming he might need a snack later. All I could think of was the episode from the television show *Seinfeld* when mutton was placed in napkins and stuffed in Jerry's jacket pockets. The dogs of New York City were following Elaine down the street as she wore Jerry's jacket on the cool evening. I could imagine the owners taking their pampered DC dogs for a walk and having to apologize as they chased after Mrs. Beam and the aromatic pocketbook strapped over her arm.

After a few hours of sightseeing, which included Ford's Theatre, Kathy and I began to think of lunch. Mr. Beam, to no one's surprise, was not hungry, so we decided to once again split up for a while and meet back at the hotel midafternoon. The MXDC Cocina Mexicana was a stylish venue, and we enjoyed the pricey but tasty Mexican fare. As we strolled back to the hotel, we noticed that the sidewalk was barricaded, and security personnel were just inside the barricades that led to three large buses. The Lions were making their way to take on the Redskins, and fans were gathering on the sidewalks asking for autographs or waving at their favorite Lion. Kathy and I strolled up from the west and decided to watch the proceedings. I mean, we were blocked anyway, so why not?

As we got a little closer, we noticed that on the first row, next to the barricade on the opposite side from us, were Mr. and Mrs. Beam. They were both just smiling and having a good time. Then it happened. I don't know if he suddenly had a hunger pang or if he decided he wanted to taunt the players, but Mr. Beam reached into the purse and pulled out a piece of bacon. He grabbed it like a stick of beef jerky and bit off a large bite.

"Hey, that's the guy from the breakfast bar," a large Lion roared. "Look, he is still eating bacon."

That ain't cool," said another.

Before long, many members of the Pride of Lions were staring at Mr. Beam, pointing at him, drooling from the sight and smell of the bacon. Mr. Beam could not hear what they were talking about and just smiled, waved back to what he considered his newfound friends, and bit into another piece of bacon. Moments later, the buses pulled away with Lions pointing and snarling at Mr. Beam and Mr. Beam smiling, waving back, and chewing.

The Lions led for most of the game that evening. The Redskins beat them with a fourth-quarter drive. The team nutritionist for Detroit mentioned after the game that he felt a lack of protein and monounsaturated fats in the diet led to an overall lack of endurance from stored energy in the players' systems, which contributed to the last-second loss. All I could do was shake my head.

Mr. Beam and the White House Squirrel

I suppose the title of this story is a bit misleading. It is technically not *the* White House squirrel, the famous pet of President Theodore Roosevelt that lived inside the White House with the first family in the early 1900s. Technically, this is *a* White House squirrel that, along with its ancestors, had been banished to the grounds when the William Taft family arrived on the scene. At least the then First Lady Nellie Taft had the good foresight to help arrange for the over three thousand Japanese cherry trees to be planted around Washington, providing a beautiful canopy for the squirrels to play for years to come.

Anyway, it had to happen. No trip anywhere with Mr. Beam could be complete without a confrontation from his greatest adversary, the bushy-tailed master of backyard disaster, the squirrel. The photo tucked away from the trip is a reminder of that brief but interesting encounter. Positioned on the south side of the White House at the top of the Ellipse, Mr. and Mrs. Beam peered toward the famous structure, wondering whom they might see. It was later afternoon, and Mr. Beam had just reached into the lunchbox, also known as Mrs. Beam's purse, and secured another piece of bacon to consume.

Slowing down the replay button in my memory of the next few moments and attempting to share the precise sequence is a bit of a challenge. Like the movie *Vantage Point*, things appear quite different depending on where you are standing. For example, Mr. Beam and

Mrs. Beam were standing close to the sagging chain between the posts of the sidewalk comprised of large gray tiles. I was standing near the backyard of the White House, peering between the wrought iron sections, measuring around six feet atop a concrete foundation. The Beams were some ten feet behind me (well, Mrs. Beam was ten feet, and of course Mr. Beam was a few paces farther back). As Mr. Beam lifted the strip of pork to his mouth, a portion of the well-done snack broke away and headed toward Earth. The hands of Mr. Beam (never to be confused with Bruce Lee when it comes to speed) began frantically trying to catch the crumb in midair. Gravity won the moment as the bacon smacked the sidewalk.

At that moment, the nearby birds began to fly toward the scene aggressively. From the corner of my eye, I beheld scampering from the beautiful green lawn of the nation's most storied estate, a squirrel squeezing through the fence, scampering onto the sidewalk, and darting toward the potential snack. Mr. Beam, not wanting to be thought of as a litterbug, began the task of bending over to pick up the bacon. With all the precision of a rusty piece of farm equipment, he leaned forward to the cacophony of popping bones. Meanwhile, with two barely noticeable twitches of the tail, the squirrel reached full speed, dashed with boldness, and grabbed the bacon, causing a startled Mr. Beam to jump almost two full inches off the ground. The squirrel leaped off of the curb just beside the sidewalk and, while posturing itself on its hind limbs, looked up holding the pork strip pressed between his two front paws. Its large round eyes stared directly at Mr. Beam, awaiting a possible counterploy for the bacon. Mr. Beam's beady little eyes stared back as if he was telekinetically about to snatch it from the squirrel. The stare-down lasted a few moments.

As I was transfixed on the comical action, a black-suited man with dark sunglasses appeared from the shadow of the trees surrounding the White House lawn. He brushed my shoulder as he quickly dashed the steps to the disturbance now drawing the attention of many bystanders.

"Sir," he said, "you cannot feed the squirrels or even birds this close to the White House." Mr. Beam countered with the "it slipped out of my hands" routine, but the black suit was not buying what Mr. Beam was selling.

By this time, a couple of bicycle policemen had gathered around. The squirrel was now enjoying the bacon, and Mr. Beam was laughing at the whole incident while the black suit was saying something like, "You think this is funny? What if that was poison you were feeding the squirrel, and it died on the White House lawn and the president came in contact with it? We have to guard against everything." He then turned to discuss things with the two officers. I suppose they could not come up with enough to hold him as, once again, Mr. Beam's smile and cabana-boy charm get him off the hook.

So, there it was again. No, not the hair spray incident at the airports but the continuous pattern of breaking rules, causing security personnel everywhere to question and try to figure out the mild-mannered man known as Mr. Beam. With this particular incident, the second favorite son-in-law kept his mouth shut, took the photos, and smiled as the bacon-eating squirrel returned to its lawn, the man in the black suit headed back to the shadows, the two policemen pointed their bikes toward the Washington Monument, and Mr. Beam reached into Mrs. Beam's purse for another piece of bacon.

Knowing Mr. Beam

(This is a trick test. Very few of the answers are in this book. This is just a few more interesting tidbits about Mr. Beam.)

Now it is question-and-answer time about how well you know the amazing Mr. Beam.

1. What is Mr. Beam's favorite movie?
   A. *The Three Amigos*
   B. *The Three Musketeers*
   C. *The Three Stooges*
   D. *Three Days of the Condor*

2. What is Mr. Beam's favorite kind of jelly?
   A. Blackberry
   B. Orange marmalade
   C. Apple
   D. Any jelly

3. Mr. Beam grew up in what community close to Albertville?
   A. Aroney
   B. Asbury
   C. Martling
   D. Hustleville

4. Mr. Beam retired from what line of work?
   A. Law enforcement
   B. Banking
   C. Music Ministry
   D. Poultry industry

5. What is Mr. Beam's favorite color?
   A. Red
   B. Blue
   C. Green
   D. Orange
   E. None; he is color-blind

6. Mr. Beam once ______
   A. Carried a dead rattlesnake in a bag on a bus from Chattanooga to Albertville.
   B. Ate six boiled eggs in three minutes trying to be like "Cool Hand Luke."
   C. Collected a jar full of lightning bugs and released them in his sister's bedroom at night.
   D. All of the above.

7. What business did Mr. Beam manage while living in Tennessee?
   A. A grocery store
   B. A funeral home
   C. A printing shop
   D. A shoe store

8. How did Mr. Beam get to school in his high school days?
   A. Walked (in the snow, uphill, both ways)
   B. Hitched a ride
   C. A tractor with a trailer on the back
   D. 1939 Ford
   E. 1941 Buick Super 127

9. What was Mr. Beam's favorite place to skinny-dip as a youth?
   A. Whippoorwill Creek.
   B. Scarham Creek
   C. Short Creek
   D. Drum Creek
   E. Leo Johnson's Creek
   F. Old Man Kelsey's Creek

10. What is Mr. Beam's favorite nickname for Mrs. Beam?
   A. Sweet momma
   B. Sally
   C. Susie
   D. Jane

***

Answers

1. (c) I should have probably stopped everything here. All I can do is shake my head. He loves them.

2. (b) This is technically correct; it is his favorite. But if you put *a*, *c*, or *d*, give yourself half credit.

3. (d) He grew up on Martling Road but almost at Hustleville Road, near the intersection close to Leo Johnson's store.

4. (d) Mr. Beam at one time worked for American Credit and was a strong-arm, tough guy who had to repossess cars. I just cannot see that. I guess he could not for too long either. He retired from Wayne Poultry as a supervisor.

5. (b) Blue it is. If his truck is any indication, then it is a very bright blue.

6. (a) He still cannot explain why he did this. He can only recall that he did it. He had killed it at a cousin's house on

a visit. Must have been a macho thing. I am just glad the person sitting next to him did not peek into the bag.

7. (a) He also tells stories of how his sweet tooth started in the grocery business. When cookie packages got damaged, he would devour the box and not even bring any home for Mrs. Beam. He told us this on the way to Annapolis. Mrs. Beam never knew this until the trip and was not happy that he never once thought to bring a damaged box home to share. For the next couple of days, he rubbed his shoulder at the spot where the punch landed.

8. (d) He probably wished it was a 1941 Buick Super, but apparently, the 1939 Ford did the trick. He says he wished he still had that one.

9. (b) He swam at the old Red Mill. I am saying Scarham Creek is the best answer, but if you said Whippoorwill Creek, give yourself partial credit. The two creeks converge at the Red Mill and form the continuation of Scarham Creek. It was here that Mr. Beam turned into the human prune. It seems another group came upon Mr. Beam swimming in the buff, and he had to wait for them to leave to get out of the creek and get his clothes. If you said Old Man Kelsey's Creek, that was Ernest T. Bass of *The Andy Griffith Show* fame. I can understand your confusion. There are similarities, but Mr. Beam is not in danger of being a precision rock thrower.

10. (d) "Sweet Momma" is the car tag, but his words are all about *Jane*. Not sure why, but one of his favorite things to say when Mrs. Beam is pulling the desserts away from his reach is, "I'm gonna konk you, Jane." She responds with, "You just better watch it." That seems to settle the issue.

Assuming each correct answer is worth ten points and the partials worth five, this is where you are as a Mr. Beam follower:

50 and below: That is a good, safe distance. You have not been negatively influenced to the point of no return. There is still hope.

50–65: Seek counseling before it is too late. 'Tis a slippery slope you tread.

66–80: You obviously know a family member, are a family member, or go to church with a family member.

81–90: Fair warning, put down this book and read something else.

91–100: Congratulations! You get to play the lead in the upcoming Mr. Beam movie.

Epilogue

At the conclusion of this writing, the family is still doing well. Mr. and Mrs. Beam continue to demonstrate a great relationship with each other and for all to see, a relationship built on their faith in God and lives that touch others through their love for their Savior, Jesus Christ. They cover us, their family, with prayers. I consider myself a very lucky man. I was raised to be independent and to decide for myself what I wanted, but also, in those choices, to choose wisely. I chose Jesus as my Savior at the age of fifteen and then chose Kathy as my wife a few years later. I had no idea what an interesting life it would be as we combined our families. I wish for you a life of love, joy, and laughter as you look to God for the answers to this sometimes crazy life. May God bless you!

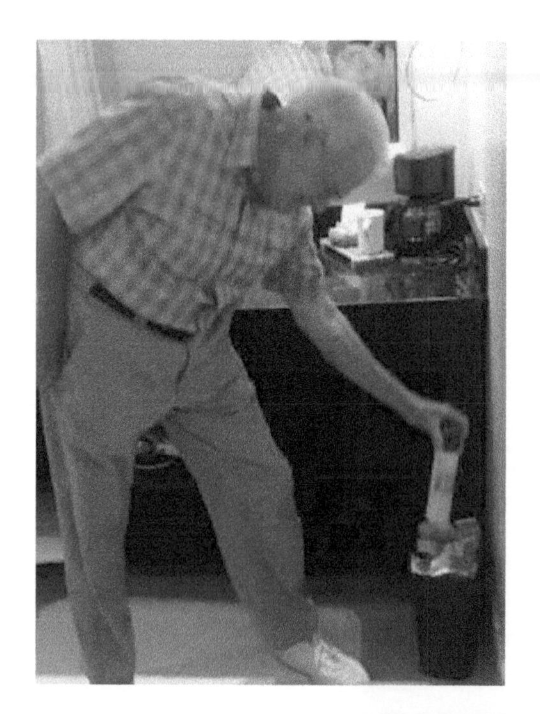